Reveal the Magic of the Microwave

Reveal the Magic of the Microwave

Chrissie Taylor

W. FOULSHAM AND CO. LTD.

London • New York • Toronto • Cape Town • Sydney

W. Foulsham & Company Limited
Yeovil Road, Slough, Berkshire, SL1 4JH

ISBN 0–572–01491–0

Printed in Great Britain by St Edmundsbury Press Limited
Bury St Edmunds, Suffolk

PREFACE

Even before qualifying as a Home Economist at Westminster Technical College in 1972 it was my ambition to write a book related to my most loved passion – catering. I have always enjoyed inventing recipes, putting ideas into action and giving my cookery appliances a special place in my kitchen. When I became a microwave owner three years ago it was a challenge to discover its powers beyond being a time-saver and cutting down on the washing-up.

I now have discovered some of its magic powers and I take this opportunity to share them with you. So many microwave books only give recipes. I hope this book will teach you much more and reveal the hidden potential of the 'Magic Box' which deserves a special place in the 20th-century kitchen. My microwave has become more than an appliance – it is an essential friend in the the fast-moving world in which we live.

Thanks to Mum, Dad, Liz and Chris for their encouragement. To Bruce for his understanding and support in writing this book.

For my daughter Sophie with love

CONTENTS

USEFUL INFORMATION

* All the processes and recipes in this publication have been tested by the author using a 700 watt microwave cooker. It is essential that the directions are followed precisely and that all of the manufacturer's instructions are strictly adhered to. The author can accept no responsibility for the outcome should the user fail to do this.

* The Ministry of Agriculture, Fisheries and Food have issued a statement explaining that as they cannot provide an accurate answer as to what degree Clingfilm is harmful in a microwave cooker, the use of clingfilm should be left to the discretion of the user.

In future, clingfilm that does contain the harmful DEHA plasticiser, used to make clingfilm stretchy, will state what the film can be used for. If there are no instructions, it should not be used for microwave cooking.

Examples of clingfilm that do not contain the DEHA plasticiser are Purecling and Saran Wrap. Roast-a-bags are also safe to use.

* For very short cooking times, if you do not have a digital timer on your microwave cooker, check the timing by using the second hand of a watch, timer or clock.

* It is important that either metric or imperial measures are followed in all recipes, not a combination of both.

* Spoon measures
1 level tablespoon – 15 ml
1 level teaspoon – 5 ml
Spoon measurements in all recipes are level.

* When herbs are used in a recipe, the flavour of dried is stronger than fresh, so use half the quantity of dried. (Unless stated otherwise, dried herbs are used in all the recipes in this book.)

TEN TEMPTING THOUGHTS

1. Washing-up is cut to a minimum as many foods can be prepared and served in the same dish.

2. Individual tastes are catered for in much less time.

3. There is no need for waste when owning a microwave as reheating of leftovers is so easy and there is only minimal loss of flavour.

4. When cooking whole cuts of meat, e.g. chops, steaks, joints, poultry, there is less shrinkage.

5. Vegetables retain more of their nutrients and have a better texture than when conventionally cooked as less water is used.

6. Slightly stale or soft foods can be refreshed or re-crisped in the microwave, e.g., cereals, bread, coffee beans, etc.

7. Warm plates in the microwave, with a small jug of water to absorb some of the microwave energy – it saves turning the oven on!

8. Heat baby bottles and food quickly and without fuss at odd hours.

9. The microwave is so versatile it can be wheeled on a trolley into the garden to warm rolls, drinks and half cook food for barbecues.

10. Dry flowers between sheets of kitchen paper, to preserve their beautiful appearance. Remember to place a glass of water in the cooker before microwaving.

TEN BASIC TIPS

1. Food cooked dry or with very little liquid, e.g. whole fish or chicken portions, should be placed in a dish relative to their size and with a well-fitting lid to retain moisture.

2. Never cook high fat or sugar content foods in plastic containers unless recommended by the manufacturers.

3. Place thinner parts of food towards the centre of the dish, thicker and more dense pieces towards the outside.

4. Bone in meat conducts heat, so cooking the meat next to the bone first. A boneless cut of meat cooks much more evenly, so whenever possible remove bones.

5. Stir soups, sauces and casseroles during cooking to ensure an even distribution of heat. If stirring food is impossible, rotate the dish two or three times during cooking.

6. Cut ingredients into equal-sized pieces when microwaving casseroles to ensure even cooking.

7. Always stand or rest food after microwaving to complete cooking and equalize the temperature throughout the food. When in doubt always undercook.

8. Occasionally sparking may occur, when small amounts of food are microwaved. Stop the cooker immediately and place a small cup of water in the cooker with the food. Some of the microwave energy will be transferred to heat the water and cooking can be continued safely.

9. Food taken from the refrigerator will take longer to cook than that at room temperature, especially during the summer or warm weather.

10. Follow your nose: when you begin to smell the food cooking it has probably had sufficient time in the microwave.

TEN REHEATING RULES

1. Always pierce clingfilm or roll back at one edge, otherwise it will explode.

2. Place thinner parts of food towards the centre of the dish and cover with gravy or sauce if possible to ensure that they do not dry out.

3. Cover food to be reheated with vented or pierced clingfilm, kitchen paper, greaseproof paper or a microwave lid according to the type of food to be reheated.

4. Dishes containing one ingredient will reheat more evenly than a combination of foods.

5. To reheat an average meal, cover with pierced clingfilm, plate or microwave lid and cook on 100% High for 3 – 3½ minutes. For more than one meal add approximately 1½ minutes to the cooking time.

6. Never reheat more than two plates of food sitting directly on top of each other, as the air passage will be restricted. Use microwave plate stacking rings for safety and do not reheat more than three meals at a time.

7. After reheating, place your hand underneath the centre of the plate or dish: if it is hot, the food is fully reheated.

8. Rotate dishes or plates of food during reheating to distribute the heat evenly.

9. Stir or toss food where possible during reheating to distribute the heat evenly, e.g. warming casseroles or stews, custards, sauces, soups, vegetables, etc.

10. Fruit and vegetables will reheat more quickly and retain moisture if they are three-quarter covered.

CONVENTIONAL RECIPE CONVERSION

Many conventional recipes can be cooked in the microwave. The most difficult factor in their success is judging the correct timing. As a guide:

1. Reduce the cooking time to a quarter of the conventional cooking time when using 100% High power level.

2. Reduce the cooking time by half when using 50% Medium power level.

3. Reduce the cooking time to three-quarters of the conventional cooking time when using Low (Defrost).

4. Add more thickening agent or reduce the liquid by a quarter especially when cooking casseroles.

Other factors to help in your recipe conversions are listed throughout the A – Z book, e.g. cakes, seasonings, fruit juice in crumbles, etc.

Remember to make a note of the quantities used, the power level and the cooking time so that you do not have to convert the recipe again.

REDUCING/INCREASING MICROWAVE RECIPES

As in conventional recipe conversion, the most difficult factor when reducing or increasing a recipe is the timing.

REDUCING

1. Choose a smaller dish.

2. If halving a recipe, microwave for approximately two-thirds of the original time. If quartering, microwave for approximately one-third of the original time.

3. Check food to see if cooked before end of calculated cooking time. Overcooked food cannot be rectified.

4. Reduce the standing time accordingly.

5. Do not reduce recipes with a high fat and sugar content as they will burn.

6. If microwaving very small amounts of food, e.g. chocolate, place a small glass of water in the cooker to absorb some of the microwave energy.

INCREASING

1. When increasing a recipe by one-half, increase the cooking time by one-third.

2. When doubling a recipe, increase the cooking time by one-half.

3. Place the food in a larger dish.

4. Increase the standing time accordingly.

5. Check food to see if it is cooked before the end of the calculated cooking time.

MICROWAVE POWER CONVERSION

All the recipes and tips in this book have been tried and tested using a 700 watt microwave cooker.

For a 600 watt microwave add 20 seconds per minute to the cooking time when using fresh ingredients.

For a 500 watt microwave add 40 seconds per minute to the cooking time when using fresh ingredients.

When reheating cooked or tinned foods add a few seconds to the total time for all the lower wattage cookers. Recipes and tips using 50% Medium power level are best cooked on 100% High for slightly less time if you do not own a variable power microwave. To adapt the timings to a lower wattage cooker, use the following table:

TIMING

650/700 watt		600 watt		500 watt	
Mins	Secs	Mins	Secs	Mins	Secs
	15		20		25
	45	1	–	1	15
1	–	1	20	1	40
2	–	2	40	3	20
3	–	4	–	5	–
4	–	5	20	6	40
5	–	6	40	8	20
6	–	8	–	10	–
7	–	9	20	11	40
8	–	10	40	13	20
9	–	12	–	15	–
10	–	13	20	16	40

A

ALMONDS

BLANCHING

Pour 225 ml (8 fl oz) boiling water over 125 g (4 oz) whole almonds in their skins. Microwave uncovered on 100% High for 1 minute. Drain and cool slightly. The skins can then be removed by squeezing each nut between the finger and thumb. Spread on kitchen paper and leave to dry.

TOASTING

Place 125 g (4 oz) skinned almonds (whole or split) in a dish with 25 g (1 oz) butter. Cover and microwave on 100% High for 2 minutes, tossing frequently to result in even browning.

APPLES

Dessert and cooking apples are cooked successfully in the microwave. Stewed and baked apples maintain their shape and colour well and need little or no additional liquid due to the high water content of the fruit.

BAKED

Wash, dry and core the fruit. Pierce the skin a few times with a fork or score round the centre. Place in a round casserole dish and stuff the middle of each apple with filling. Cover and microwave on 100% High. Four apples will take 7–9 minutes, depending on their size. Leave to stand for 5 minutes, spoon over juices and serve with custard or whipped cream.

For fillings, choose one of the following:

Mincemeat   Ready-made mincemeat is ideal and timesaving. Use 1 tbsp for each apple.

Orange   Mix together 1 tbsp each of chopped nuts, brown sugar, sultanas, currants, desiccated coconut. Bind with the grated rind and juice of 1 orange.

Spiced   Mix together 1 tbsp each of brown sugar, sultanas and chopped dates with ½ tsp nutmeg or mixed spice. Bind with the grated rind and juice of 1 lemon.

SAUCE

To make a speedy apple sauce, peel, core and chop 450 g (1 lb) fruit and place in a bowl with 15 g (½ oz) unsalted butter or margarine and ¼ tsp ground cloves. Cover and microwave on 100% High for 8 minutes. Mash to a pulp and serve hot or cold as an accompaniment to pork, e.g. roast, chops, steaks, sausages, escalopes. The cloves may be omitted and the skin left on the apples if preferred.

STEWED

Choose unblemished and firm fruit. A crisp apple is more suitable for pie filling as the slices hold their shape better. Peel, core and slice 450 g (1 lb) fruit evenly and place in a deep dish.

Mix together 75 g (3 oz) granulated or brown sugar with 2 tbsp water, 1 tbsp lemon juice and 1 tsp spice of your choice, e.g. nutmeg, cinnamon, mixed spice.

Spread over apples and toss to coat well. Cover and microwave on 100% High for 6–8 minutes, stirring once halfway through cooking time. Leave to stand for 2 minutes before serving. If the stewed apple is for pie filling, uncover after cooking and leave to cool. If stewing dessert apples, reduce the amount of sugar accordingly.

APRICOTS

DRIED

It is not necessary to soak dried apricots overnight before cooking them in the microwave, although soaking achieves a slightly better result. Place 225 g (8 oz) in a bowl with 600 ml (1 pt) water. Cover with a lid and microwave on 100% High for 15 minutes, stirring once during cooking. Leave to stand for 10 minutes and use as required.

For a more interesting flavour substitute unsweetened fruit juice for half the water. Thicken any remaining juice with cornflour, sweeten with sugar and use as a sauce for puddings, sponges, ice-cream and fruit.

PEELING

Microwave each fresh apricot for 5–10 seconds on 100% High. Stand for 30 seconds before removing the skin.

POACHING

Pierce skins or prick with a fork to prevent them from bursting if cooking whole. Place 450 g (1 lb) fruit in a bowl with 1 tbsp water and microwave on 100% High for 3–4 minutes. Stir once during cooking if the fruit is stoned and halved. Stand for 3 minutes. Serve hot with a liqueur syrup sauce, blanched almonds or fresh cream.

If using to fill flans, poach the apricots whole to retain their shape. Cool, halve and remove stones.

PURÉEING

Cook as if poaching. When cool, place the fruit in a liquidizer or food processor with enough sugar syrup to give a thick pouring consistency. Serve as a sauce for ice-cream, sweet puddings and sponges or as an accompaniment for gammon and bacon.

See *Sugar Syrup*

ASPARAGUS

Fresh asparagus cooks so much better in a microwave than when conventionally cooked. As so little water is used, its rich colour is maintained and the full flavour of the vegetable can be appreciated.

Choose stalks of similar thickness and length if possible, so that they will cook evenly. Trim the ends off 450 g (1 lb) and arrange the stalks in a shallow dish with the spears pointing towards the centre. Sprinkle with 2–4 tbsp water, cover with pierced clingfilm and microwave on 100% High for 6–7 minutes until just tender but crisp. Stand for 2 minutes. Drain and serve with a glaze of melted butter or lemon butter and a garnish of lemon slices. Sprinkle with sesame seeds or blanched split almonds.

See *Butter*, *Flavoured*, and *Almonds*

AUBERGINES

Aubergines are cooked quickly in the microwave without any risk of discoloration.

SLICES

Cook aubergine for moussaka by placing 450 g (1 lb) slices in a casserole with 4 tbsp boiling water. Cover with pierced clingfilm and microwave on 100% High for 6–8 minutes, tossing twice during cooking. Stand for 3 minutes.

Microwave a prepared moussaka to serve four on 100% High for 10–12 minutes, turning the dish once during cooking. Stand for 3 minutes. Brown under a hot grill or garnish with sliced tomato and parsley.

WHOLE

Wash and trim the ends of 450g (1 lb) aubergines. Prick the skins and brush with oil. Place on a sheet of kitchen paper and microwave on 100% High for 4–5 minutes, rearranging and turning once during cooking. Stand for 3 minutes.

The aubergines are ready to use in your favourite stuffed aubergine recipe. After filling, arrange in a dish, cover and microwave on 100% High for 6–7 minutes, turning once during cooking. Stand for 3 minutes and serve with tomato sauce if liked.

See *Sauces*, *Tomato*

B

BABIES' FOOD

BOTTLES

Babies bottles cannot be sterilized using a microwave cooker. Use a proprietary sterilizing agent for their specialized care.

JARS

Remove metal caps, cover loosely with clingfilm and microwave on 100% High for 15–30 seconds. Stir and serve straight from the jar.

MILK

Heat 200 ml (7 fl oz) milk in a sterilized baby's bottle (teat and covering cap may be left on) for 30–45 seconds. Reconstituted baby milk may also be reheated in the microwave.

BACON

The microwave is an excellent method for cooking bacon with less shrinkage, no splattering and better shape retention than when conventionally cooked. Place a sheet of kitchen paper on a plate or dish and arrange layers of bacon rashers, overlapping fat and lean meat. Cover with another sheet of kitchen paper to avoid the fat spitting during cooking. Microwave on 100% High for 30–60 seconds per rasher, rotating the dish halfway through cooking time if several rashers are being cooked. Leave to stand for 2 minutes for evenly cooked, crisp rashers.

Thick slices and smoked rashers will take slightly longer to cook than thin or unsmoked rashers.

Bacon may also be cooked on a browning dish or roasting rack, following the manufacturer's instructions.

BANANAS

BAKED

Peel and split two large bananas lengthways, then cut in half (eight pieces). Place a single layer in a round dish and sprinkle with 4 tbsp orange and lemon juice and 1 tbsp brown sugar. Microwave on 100% High for 3 minutes. Serve hot with cream. Substitute 1 tbsp rum for 1 tbsp juice for a more exciting flavour.

BEETROOT

The microwave is an excellent timesaver when cooking this root crop. Place 450 g (1 lb) washed, even-sized beetroot in a bowl with 4 tbsp water. Microwave on 100% High for 5–7 minutes, tossing twice during cooking. Cool, then remove the skins with finger and thumb.

BEVERAGES

Heat one cup or mug of tea, coffee, chocolate, milk, etc. on 100% High for 1½–2 minutes.

BISCUITS

BASES

Bases for cheesecakes are easily made using the microwave. Melt 75 g (3 oz) unsalted butter and add one of the following crushed biscuits: 175 g (6 oz) plain digestives, chocolate digestives, ginger or rich tea biscuits. Mix well and press into a 18 cm (7 inch) dish. Useful as a topping for fruit fools and mousses.

See *Butter, melting*

RE-CRISPING

To re-crisp crackers and biscuits without fillings (e.g. not custard creams), place a sheet of kitchen paper on the base of the cooker and arrange a layer in a circle. Microwave on 100% High for a few seconds. Cool and store in an airtight container.

BLACKBERRIES

See *Fruit*

BOTTLING

FRUIT

Method and timing for one 500 ml (18 fl oz) jar. Microwave jars of fruit individually.

Pack the prepared fruit into a warmed sterilized jar and pour in the hot syrup. Cover with clingfilm. Microwave on 100% High for 2–3 minutes, then on (Low) Defrost for 3–4 minutes.

Use oven gloves to remove from the cooker. Cover, seal and label. The fruit will keep for up to two months.

See *Sterilizing*

BREAD

BAKING

When bread making, warm flour for 15 seconds on 100% High to assist in proving and rising dough.

Place dough in a lightly floured bowl. Cover and microwave on Low (Defrost) for 15 seconds. Stand for 10 minutes. Repeat until dough has doubled in size.

Microwaved bread doughs dry out much quicker than when conventionally cooked. To help prevent this, when cool wrap in a sealed polythene bag or plastic container.

As microwaved dough does not brown, sprinkle with sesame seeds, poppy seeds, bran, oats, or crushed grains before cooking. Recipes that use brown flours, sugar or eggs in the ingredients will look more appealing when cooked.

DEFROSTING

Cut loaves May be left in the wrapping but remove any metal clip or seal. Microwave on Low (Defrost) for 5 minutes. If only a few slices are required, wrap in kitchen paper and microwave on 100% High for 8–12 seconds.

Uncut loaves Wrap in kitchen paper to absorb the moisture and microwave on 100% High for 1½–2 minutes. A hard lump will remain in the centre, so stand for 5 minutes to finish the defrosting process. Bread will toughen if allowed to overheat.

Rolls, buns, scones, etc. Do not microwave in plastic bags. Wrap in kitchen paper and microwave on Low (Defrost) for approximately 8 seconds each. For several rolls, place them in a ring on a sheet of kitchen paper and cover with another piece. Microwave as above, adjusting the time accordingly.

Teabreads Can also be defrosted using this process. Reduce the time slightly according to the size of the loaf.

REFRESHING

Cut bread into slices and wrap in kitchen paper. Microwave on 100% High for 5–10 seconds for six slices.

FRENCH BREAD

Cheese   Cut the loaf into thick slices to within 1 cm (½ inch) of the base so leaving the loaf intact. Place alternate slices of processed Cheddar and Emmenthal cheese between the incisions. Place on a piece of kitchen paper and microwave on 50% Medium for 1–1½ minutes until the cheese has started to melt.

Serve with quiche, soups and salads.

Garlic   Cut loaf as above. Cream 125 g (4 oz) butter with 4 crushed garlic cloves and 1 tsp chopped parsley. Spread between the slices, wrap loosely in kitchen paper and microwave on 100% High for 1–1½ minutes.

Serve with soups and lasagne.

Herb   Substitute 1 tbsp fresh or dried herbs for garlic cloves.

FRENCH TOAST

Beat two eggs, 25 g (1 oz) melted butter and 2 tbsp milk together. Cut bread or French stick into 2.5 cm (1 inch) slices and dip in the egg mixture. Prepare a browning dish and microwave the toast on 100% High for ½–1 minute. Turn over and cook for a further ½–1 minute until browned.

If making sweet toast, add 1 tsp icing sugar and a pinch of nutmeg or cinnamon to the egg mixture.

If making savoury toast, add a pinch of salt and pepper to the mixture. Serve with breakfast foods or as a snack.

FRIED BREAD

Remove the crusts of two slices of brown or white bread. Butter on both sides, place on a shallow dish and microwave on 100% High for 40–60 seconds. Turn over and cook for 40–60 seconds. Top with scrambled or poached egg or tomatoes. A better result will be achieved if a browning dish is used.

PITTA BREAD

Warm pitta bread in the microwave to serve with soups, pâtés or dips. Wrap in kitchen paper and microwave on 100% High for a few seconds. As a tasty snack, split and fill the breads with ham, cheese, tomatoes, or chopped crisp salad vegetables. Place on a double layer of kitchen paper and microwave on 100% High for 45–60 seconds.

TOASTED SANDWICHES

Using the egg mixture for French toast (above), make up sweet or savoury sandwiches and dip in the batter. Prepare a browning dish and microwave one sandwich on 100% High for 1 minute. Turn over and cook for 1 minute more.

Alternatively, butter two slices of fresh crusty bread and make a sandwich with the filling between the unbuttered sides. Prepare a browning dish and microwave each side of the sandwich on 100% High for 30–45 seconds.

Serve as a tasty, quick snack.

See *Croissants*

BREADCRUMBS

Lay slices of brown or white bread on an upturned cardboard egg box for support and to assist the drying process evenly. Microwave on 100% High for 1–1½ minutes per slice. Leave until cold and the slices will crumb easily. Stale bread absorbs cooking juices much more than fresh.

BROWNING

Breadcrumbs are easily browned in the microwave to be used as a topping for casseroles and desserts or as a coating for fish, poultry and chops. Crumb 50 g (2 oz) brown or white bread including crusts in a processor or blender. Spread on kitchen paper and microwave on 100% High for 5–7 minutes until completely dry, tossing two or three times during cooking. Cool and store in an airtight container for up to six weeks.

FLAVOURING

To flavour browned or toasted breadcrumbs, add 1–2 tbsp parsley, thyme, chilli or curry powder, garlic salt, celery salt, microwave seasonings, dried citrus zest etc. Crushed wheat crackers, crushed cream crackers, oats, wheatflakes, sesame seeds, poppy seeds or coconut can be mixed with breadcrumbs for variety and used for a coating.

Use to coat skinned chicken joints, bacon steaks, escalopes, pork and lamb chops, or as a garnish and decoration for vegetables and desserts.

TOASTING

Place 25 g (1 oz) unsalted butter or margarine in a bowl and melt on 100% High for 1 minute. Add 125 g (4 oz) seasoned white breadcrumbs and mix together well. Spread half the mixture on a 20 cm (8 inch) plate and cook uncovered for 1 minute on 100% High. Stir to bring the outside browning crumbs into the centre and microwave on 100% High for 1 minute more. Repeat this process for the remaining breadcrumbs.

BROCCOLI

Try to choose heads and stalks of a uniform size. Trim the ends from 225 g (8 oz) broccoli and arrange in a shallow dish with the heads pointing towards the centre. Sprinkle with 4 tbsp water and cover with pierced clingfilm. Microwave on 100% High for 6–8 minutes, giving the dish a half turn once during cooking time. Leave to stand for 2 minutes. Drain and serve with lemon butter, and a sprinkling of toasted almonds or sesame seeds.

See *Butter, Flavoured*

BROWNING AGENTS

There are a variety of browning agents that can be used to improve the appearance of meats during cooking.

Brush with soy sauce, Worcestershire sauce combined with water and melted butter, gravy browning, honey, paprika, microwave seasoning, brown onion soup mix (reconstituted), honey, brown and fruity sauces, barbecue sauce etc.

Whenever possible use unsalted butter as salt can toughen food fibres, especially when cooking meat.

For recipes, see *Butter, Flavoured* and *Meat Glazes and Bastes*.

BROWNING DISHES

See *Dishes*

BRUSSELS SPROUTS

Cooking sprouts in the microwave gives particularly good results. They retain their crispness and colour and odours are cut to a minimum.

Wash and remove the outer leaves of 450 g (1 lb) sprouts and cut a small cross at the base. Place in a bowl with 4 tbsp water, cover and microwave for 6–7 minutes, tossing once during cooking.

Stand for 2–3 minutes, drain, season and serve with a sauce or lemon butter.

See *Butter*, *Flavoured* and *Sauces*

BUTTER

Whenever possible use unsalted butter in a baste as salt will toughen the food, especially when cooking meat.

BROWNING

Place 125 g (4 oz) butter in a heatproof dish. Cover and microwave on 100% High for 5–6 minutes, stirring three times during cooking. Skim off any foam and use to glaze vegetables to enhance their colour and appearance.

CLARIFYING

To clarify salted butter place 50 g (2 oz) in a bowl and cover with greaseproof paper to prevent spitting. Microwave on 100% High for 1 minute. The sediment can then be removed.
See *Fat*

FLAVOURED

Anchovy   Melt 50 g (2 oz) unsalted butter, add 25 g (1 oz) drained and mashed anchovy fillets, 1 tbsp chopped parsley, black pepper and squeeze of lemon juice. Use as a glaze for fish.

Cheese Melt 50 g (2 oz) unsalted butter. Add 1 tsp Parmesan cheese and seasoning.

Use as a glaze for whole sweetcorn. Sprinkle with parsley.

Garlic Melt 50 g (2 oz) unsalted butter. Add a few shakes of garlic powder or 2 crushed fresh garlic cloves and seasoning.

Use as a glaze for grilled steaks, chops, potatoes and courgettes.

Herb Melt 50 g (2 oz) unsalted butter. Add either 1 tsp parsley, mint, chives, thyme, etc. and seasoning.

Use as a glaze for potatoes, carrots, cauliflower, parsnips and poached fish.

Lemon or Orange Melt 50 g (2 oz) unsalted butter and add 1 tbsp lemon or orange juice and seasoning.

Use as a glaze for asparagus, broccoli, carrots or poached fish. Garnish with the grated zest.

Liqueur Soften 125 g (4 oz) unsalted butter and beat in 50 g (2 oz) sieved icing sugar and 2 tbsp brandy, rum or liqueur of your choice.

Use as a topping for Christmas pudding, rum babas, croissants, fruit flans or sponges.

A pat of savoury butter placed on cooked food improves its appearance and adds more flavour. Use the recipes above, but just soften the butter slightly instead of melting it. Place on a sheet of greaseproof paper and form into a roll. Chill in a refrigerator until hardened, then slice to garnish hot food.

See *Low Fat Spread*

MELTING

Place 25 g (1 oz) butter in a dish, cover and microwave on 100% High for 15–30 seconds.

SOFTENING

Remove the wrapper from 225 g (8 oz) butter and place in a dish. Microwave on Low (Defrost) for 1–1½ minutes and leave to stand for 2 minutes before use.

C

CABBAGE

Red, green, white, Savoy cabbage and Chinese leaves can be cooked using this method. Shred a combination of them to give a more interesting colour.

When cutting red cabbage use a stainless steel knife to stop it 'bleeding' and add 1 tsp vinegar to preserve its colour when cooking.

Serve cabbage with a basic white sauce topped with grated cheese, breadcrumbs, crisps or parsley to improve the appearance.

COOKING

Wash 450 g (1 lb) shredded cabbage and drain well. Place in a pierced boilable or roasting bag with a knob of butter. Microwave on 100% High for 6–8 minutes, tossing once during cooking. Salt, toss again and leave to stand for 2 minutes. Cabbage may also be cooked in a covered dish using the same method.

REMOVING LEAVES

The outer leaves of a cabbage are easily removed by microwaving for recipes requiring whole leaves, e.g. stuffed cabbage leaves. Simply wash the whole cabbage, place in a dish, cover and microwave on 100% High for 2–3 minutes. Approximately six outer leaves can then be removed. Repeat until required number have been loosened and blanched.

To make cabbage leaf parcels, trim away the hard centre at the base of each leaf, fill with stuffing and roll into neat parcels. Place eight in a dish with the seams underneath and cover with tomato sauce. Cover and microwave on 100% High for 8–10 minutes, turning the dish once and basting the parcel halfway through the cooking time. Stand for 3 minutes before serving. If a raw meat stuffing is used increase the cooking time accordingly.

See *Sauces* and *Stuffings*

CAKES

BASIC RULES

Do not grease and flour dishes as this will result in a hard crust forming on the outside of the cake. Instead line the dish with greaseproof paper or clingfilm or *very* lightly grease the dish but *do not* flour.

When cooking cakes, stand the dish on an upturned plate or saucer to encourage an even distribution of the microwaves.

Add custard powder to cakes or puddings to improve colour. Substitute 15 g (½ oz) custard powder for 15 g (½ oz) flour.

A cake will not spoil when the microwave door is opened, unlike conventional cooking. This means the dish can be turned frequently to ensure an even cooking of the mixture.

Microwaved sponges have a tendency to dry out. To prevent this, fill and ice when cool, wrap in foil or store in an airtight container. A stale uniced cake can be refreshed by microwaving on Low (Defrost) for 30 seconds.

Cocoa brings out the fat content in a cake mixture, making it heavy. For this reason use only 15 g (½ oz) cocoa to every 125 g (4 oz) fat.

CREAMED MIXTURES

Creamed mixtures will be lighter and have a better flavour if the butter and sugar are warmed for a few seconds before creaming.

FAIRY CAKES

To ensure that fairy cakes keep their shape during cooking if you do not have a microwave bun tray, use two cake cases or cut yoghurt pots so that cases fit inside them.

FILLINGS AND TOPPINGS

For quick and easy sponge cake fillings, use proprietary jars of spreads, e.g. hazelnut, chocolate, vanilla etc. Alternatively, use a can of pie filling to sandwich and top a sponge or fill a flan. To make a hot sauce for puddings and ice-cream, empty a can or jar of pie filling into a bowl, cover and microwave on 100% High for 2 minutes. Stir halfway through cooking time.

Another quick topping for sponges and ice-cream is a Mars Bar or some after dinner mints melted on 50% Medium for 1–2 minutes.

Decorate iced cakes with chopped nuts, flaked almonds, chocolate vermicelli, grated white, milk or plain chocolate, sieved icing sugar, cherries, glacé fruits and angelica, toasted coconut or citrus zest.

See *Icing*

Butter Cream   Place 125 g (4 oz) unsalted butter, 350 g (12 oz) sieved icing sugar and 2 tbsp milk in a bowl. Microwave on 100% High for 1 minute. Add the grated rind and juice of one orange or lemon and beat until smooth. Use to ice and fill sponge cakes. This icing may also be flavoured with liquid coffee or essences, e.g. vanilla, almond, rum, pistachio etc. Omit the juice before flavouring.

Chocolate   Place 125 g (4 oz) unsalted butter, 4 tbsp drinking chocolate powder, 300 g (10 oz) sieved icing sugar and 2 tbsp milk in a bowl. Microwave on 100% High for 3 minutes. Beat until thick and smooth. Cool. Use to fill and ice sponges and fairy cakes.

Toffee   Place 125 g (4 oz) unsalted butter, 125 g (4 oz) soft brown sugar and 1 small can of condensed milk in a bowl. Microwave uncovered on 100% High for 4 minutes, stirring once halfway through the cooking time. Remove with oven gloves and beat until smooth. Leave to cool if using to sandwich and ice cakes, or serve hot with puddings and ice-cream.

This sauce can also be poured over shortbread and when cold spread with a layer of melted chocolate to make a caramel bar.

See *Shortbread*

FRUIT CAKES

Cook fruit cakes on Low (Defrost) to develop the flavour of the ingredients. Use dark brown sugar and 1 tsp gravy browning to ensure a rich colour.

If your fruit cake recipe does not cook through to the centre, use the following tips:

1. Use small eggs and reduce the liquid content slightly.
2. Make a well in the centre before cooking.
3. Wrap the cake in foil during the standing time.

SPONGE MIXTURES

Microwaved sponge mixtures need to be slightly wetter than conventional recipes. Add an extra 2 tbsp milk or water for a lighter and moister result.

As sponges do not brown on the surface when cooked in the microwave, improve their appearance by using brown sugar, a mixture of white and brown flour, treacle, chocolate or cocoa if possible. This will not be necessary if the sponge is to be iced or decorated after cooking.

CARROTS

New baby carrots cook much better than old as they are smaller and do not have a woody core.

NEW

To cook whole, wash, top and tail 350 g (12 oz) new carrots. Place in a dish with 2 tbsp water. Cover with pierced clingfilm and microwave on 100% High for 6–8 minutes, tossing once during cooking. Stand for 3 minutes. Drain, season and serve with orange butter or white sauce.

OLD

Peel, top and tail 225 g (8 oz) old carrots and cut into 5 mm (¼ inch) slices or wedges. Microwave for 4–7 minutes. Continue as for new.

See *Butter*, *Flavoured* and *Sauces*

CASSEROLES

Cheap, tough cuts of meat are not cooked successfully in the microwave as they need very long, slow cooking to break down the fibres. When cooking casseroles choose a more tender cut than when conventionally cooking or tenderize the meat in a marinade overnight. Microwave casseroles on 100% High until the liquid is boiling, then cook on 50% Medium or less if possible.

When microwaving casseroles or stews, grease will rise to the surface. Remove with a spoon or kitchen paper during cooking.

To give a good result, cut the ingredients into even-sized pieces and stir the casserole frequently to ensure an even distribution of heat. Turn the dish regularly to assist in even cooking.

See *Marinades*

CAULIFLOWER

To cook a 450 g (1 lb) cauliflower whole, trim the outside leaves away and cut the stalk off as close as possible to the florets. Wash well but do not dry and wrap in wet greaseproof paper.

Place in a dish, stalk uppermost and microwave on 100% High for 4–5 minutes. Turn the whole cauliflower over and microwave for a further 4–5 minutes. Leave to stand for 2 minutes. Season and coat with melted butter, parsley or cheese sauce. Sprinkle with a crisp garnish.

See *Sauces* and *Garnishes*

CELERY

Microwaved celery retains its crunchy texture and golden colour.

HEARTS

Slice celery hearts in half and for each heart add 2 tbsp water. Place a single layer in a dish, cover and microwave on 100% High. Four hearts will take 5–6 minutes. Stock can be used instead of water to give a fuller flavour. Serve as below.

SLICED

Separate stalks, trim ends and wash in cold water. Slice into 1 cm (½ inch) pieces and place in a dish with 2 tbsp water and 25 g (1 oz) butter. Cover and microwave on 100% High for 4–5 minutes, tossing once during cooking. Stand for 2 minutes.

Drain and serve with a flavoured white sauce or on their own with a glaze of melted butter and black pepper.

See *Sauces* and *Butter, Flavoured*

CEREALS

To re-crisp soft cereals, spread one or two servings on a large plate lined with kitchen paper and place in the microwave with a cup of water. Depending on the staleness of the cereals, microwave on 100% High for 30 seconds to 3 minutes, tossing every 30 seconds and testing for crispness.

CHAPATIS

Reheat chapatis in the microwave. Place two on a plate and microwave on 100% High for approximately 1 minute until swollen and hot.

CHEESE

CHEESE ON TOAST

Cheese becomes softer when microwaved than grilled, but if overcooked in the microwave it will become tough and stringy. For a good result take one slice of buttered toast and top with grated or sliced cheese. Place on a sheet of kitchen paper in the centre of the cooker and microwave for 10–30 seconds.

CREAM CHEESE

Cream cheese and cheese spreads will spread easily if microwaved on Low (Defrost) for a few seconds. Remove any foil covering before microwaving.

REHEATING CHEESE DISHES

Do not reheat cheese recipes from frozen. Allow the meal to thaw first otherwise the cheese will cook before the other ingredients and could be stringy and tough. Only add cheese as a topping during the last couple of minutes of microwaving whenever possible.

RIPENING

Soft cheese can be ripened in the microwave, e.g. Camembert, Brie, Stilton.

Place 225 g (8 oz) cheese on a serving board (not wooden) and microwave on Low (Defrost) for 15–45 seconds depending on the condition of the cheese. Leave to stand for 5 minutes before serving. Harder cheeses may be brought to room temperature by using the method above and microwaved for slightly longer.

CHEESECAKES

See *Biscuits, Bases*

CHESTNUTS

SKINNING AND COOKING

Chestnuts can be skinned and cooked using the microwave. Take 225 g (8 oz) chestnuts and make a slit in their skins using a sharp knife. Place in a heatproof bowl and pour over 600 ml (1 pt) boiling water. Microwave on 100% High for 7–10 minutes, drain and cool slightly. The outer casing and skin can then be removed easily.

CREAMED

Soak 125 g (4 oz) dried chestnuts overnight. Drain and place in a bowl with 150 ml (¼ pt) boiling water. Cover with a lid and microwave on 100% High for 5 minutes, stirring once during cooking. Cool with the remaining juices and cream in a liquidizer or food processor. Use for stuffings and cake fillings.

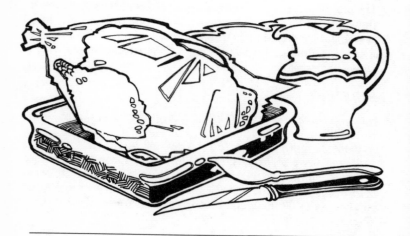

CHICKEN

Chicken cooks beautifully in the microwave, because the meat remains moist and flavoursome. However, the skin will not crisp and turn golden brown: to improve the appearance, brush the bird with a browning agent before cooking or serve coated with a sauce. Cook the chicken on an upturned saucer placed in a dish or on a roasting rack to allow the juices to run away.

Place the bird in a roasting bag, or cover with greaseproof paper to assist browning. If using a roasting bag, cut the corner off so that the juices can drain away during cooking.

Microwave breast side down for one third of the cooking time, drain the juices, turn over and continue cooking. Wrap in foil shiny side inwards, stand for 5–8 minutes. To test if the bird is cooked there should be no trace of pink when the flesh is pierced between the leg joint and breast. Use the drained juices to make a gravy or sauce.

Microwave chicken on 100% High for 6 minutes per 450 g (lb) or 50% Medium for 9 minutes per 450 g (lb).

BONED AND STUFFED

Follow the same basic rules as cooking chicken. Do not pack stuffing too tightly. Weigh the stuffed bird and calculate the cooking time for 9–10 minutes per 450 g (lb). Microwave on 100% High for the first 6 minutes then on 50% Medium for the remainder of the timing. Turn the dish frequently and drain away the juices during cooking. (A stuffed whole chicken is best microwaved on 50% Medium setting.)

BRAISED

Microwave on 100% High for 8–9 minutes per 450 g (lb).

DRUMSTICKS

Cook drumsticks unseasoned or choose a coating of bread-crumbs, stuffing mix, etc. Place eight drumsticks in a circle on a plate, prepared browning dish or roasting rack with the thinner part of the drumstick towards the centre. Microwave on 100% High for 12–14 minutes, turning over halfway through cooking.

Stand for 2–3 minutes, serve hot or cold with a sauce or relish.

See *Browning Agents, Coatings, Sauces, Meat Glazes and Bastes*

CHIPS

See *Potatoes*

CHOCOLATE

MELTING

Place 125 g (4 oz) chocolate in a bowl and microwave on 50% Medium or Low (Defrost) for 2 minutes. Stir halfway through cooking time and allow to stand for 1 minute before using. If smaller amounts than this are melted, place half a cup of water in the cooker with the chocolate to prevent possible sparking.

CHUTNEY

Chutneys can be made successfully in the microwave. The advantages are that odours are cut to a minimum, there is no condensation and they cook quickly. Follow the basic rules of making jam for safety and to ensure a good finished result.

See *Jam*

CITRUS

FRUITS

Heat oranges, lemons, limes or grapefruits in the microwave on 100% High for 30 seconds each. You will be able to extract almost twice as much juice and the fruit will be easier to squeeze.

ZEST

This is a useful ingredient to flavour sweet and savoury dishes. To dry zest in the microwave, finely grate the rind from one medium or two small oranges, lemons or limes. Spread evenly on a plate and place in the microwave with a cup of water. Cook on 100% High for 4–6 minutes until zest is dry to the touch. Check at 1 minute intervals while cooking, rubbing between fingers and thumb to separate the particles. Leave to stand until dry (at least 3 hours) and store in an airtight jar for up to two months. When using dried zest in a recipe, only half the amount is needed as for fresh.

CLINGFILM

See *Covering Food* and page 9.

COATINGS

Meat that does not brown naturally in the microwave can be sprinkled and dipped in a crunchy coating to add 'bite', extra flavour and colour. Coatings also help to keep meat moist. Brush chops, steaks, drumsticks, etc. with beaten egg, then dip into coating mixture pressing it on well. Some meats may need to be dipped in egg and coated twice to ensure that the flesh is covered. Microwave on a browning dish or rack for the usual time, turning at intervals to ensure even cooking.

If the meat is microwaved on a plate or dish do not turn over during cooking. The surface will then keep crisp.

For speed, use stuffing mixes or convenience packets of coatings. Dried breadcrumbs can also be used.

See *Breadcrumbs*

COCOA

Cocoa has a tendency to bring out the fat content in a cake mixture, making it heavy. For this reason use only 15 g (½ oz) to each 125 g (4 oz) fat.

COCONUT

To toast coconut place 25 g (1 oz) in a dish and microwave on 100% High for 1 minute, tossing several times during cooking until golden brown.

COFFEE

BEANS, REFRESHING

Coffee beans can be refreshed in the microwave to restore their aroma and taste. Put 2 tbsp in a bowl lined with kitchen paper and place in the cooker with a cup of water. Microwave on 100% High for 30 seconds, tossing halfway through cooking time. Cool, grind and use as freshly roasted beans.

MAKING PERCOLATED COFFEE

Fresh, roasted beans are best for a full flavour. Put 2 tbsp ground coffee in a heatproof jug and pour over 600 ml (1 pt) cold water, stirring well. Microwave on 100% High for 4–5 minutes until very hot but not boiling. Cover and leave to infuse for 4–5 minutes for the flavour to develop. Strain, reheat for 1 minute and serve.

REHEATING

Make a full pot of coffee in a percolator or coffee machine. Reheat a cold cup or mug of coffee as required on 100% High for 1½–2 minutes. The coffee will taste as good as freshly made.

COURGETTES

Because of their high water content, courgettes cook beautifully in the microwave without the addition of liquid. They also retain their crispness and bright colour. Wash, top and tail 450 g (1 lb) courgettes. Cut into even-sized slices and place in a dish with 25 g (1 oz) butter. Cover and microwave on 100% High for 4–6 minutes, tossing once during cooking. Season and stand for 2 minutes. Drain and serve with flavoured butter or cheese sauce.

See *Butter, Flavoured* and *Sauces*

COVERING FOOD

Covering food during microwaving prevents spattering, holds in moisture, keeping it tender and soft, and assists in shortening the cooking time. Because moisture is retained, less, little or no liquid is required during microwaving, unlike conventional cookery.

When a tight-fitting cover is required in a recipe place a sheet of greaseproof paper underneath a casserole lid.

Use a tight covering of clingfilm when cooking foods that need little or no added liquid. Pierce or roll back clingfilm at one edge when cooking foods with a high liquid content or those which produce a lot of steam. Failure to do this may cause the clingfilm to explode as the steam cannot escape. (Unless using microwave clingfilm, such as Purecling and Saran Wrap, do not let ordinary clingfilm touch food.)

Kitchen paper stops splattering, absorbs moisture and allows steam to escape. Use to cover fatty food, e.g. when cooking bacon etc. and for heating breads, etc. when the moisture of the food needs to be absorbed to keep it crisp.

Greaseproof paper also prevents splattering and is used when moisture need not be retained in the food.

Roasting bags are ideal for cooking food in the microwave. They assist in browning food and are particularly useful when cooking joints of meat and poultry. Moisture is kept inside the bag, making the food more succulent, and because no spitting can occur the inside of the cooker is kept clean. Tie the bags loosely with string or use an elastic band. When cooking meats, snip off one corner of the bag so that the juices can drain away.

CREAM

DAIRY WHIPPED

To thaw 250 ml (9 fl oz) frozen cream, remove foil lid and cover with clingfilm. Microwave on Low (Defrost) for 2½–3 minutes. Stand for 5 minutes, stir lightly and serve.

DOUBLE

Place 600 ml (1 pt) double cream pieces, portions or flakes in a bowl and microwave on Low (Defrost) for 5 minutes, turning over halfway through cooking time. Stir and stand for 5 minutes before serving.

CROISSANTS

To warm croissants, place two on a sheet of kitchen paper inside the cooker with a small glass of water. Microwave on 100% High for 30–45 seconds. The water helps to keep the croissant moist. Serve immediately with butter, jam or melted chocolate. Alternatively, split and butter a cold croissant and fill with ham, cheese, tomato or filling of your choice. Place on a sheet of kitchen paper inside the cooker and microwave on 100% High for 45–60 seconds until the filling is hot. This makes a quick tasty snack.

CROUTONS

Remove crusts from 175 g (6 oz) white, brown or wholemeal bread and dice into 1 cm (½ inch) cubes. Spread a single layer in a dish and microwave on 100% High for 3–4 minutes, tossing every minute until dry. For flavouring, toss the bread cubes with one of the following and microwave as above.

Garlic Melt 25 g (1 oz) butter with two cloves of crushed garlic or 1 tsp garlic salt.

Herb Melt 25 g (1 oz) butter, add 2 tsp mixed herbs, pinch of salt and pepper.

Parsley Melt 25 g (1 oz) butter, add 2 tsp chopped parsley, pinch of salt and pepper.

Savoury Melt 25 g (1 oz) butter, add 1 tsp chicken seasoning.

CRUMBLES

As crumbles do not brown in the microwave, use wholemeal flour and demerara sugar instead of white. Add chopped nuts for a crisp, crunchy texture.

Often the fruit juice in crumbles and puddings bubbles over during cooking. To prevent this from happening, stir in 1 tsp cornflour to every 225 g (8 oz) fruit before microwaving.

CURDS

Orange, lemon, grapefruit or lime curds are easily made in the microwave using either a conventional or microwave recipe.

To set 450 g (1 lb) of curd, place rind, juice, sugar and butter in a bowl and microwave on 100% High for 2 minutes. Stir and add the beaten eggs. Microwave on 100% High for a further 3–4 minutes, stirring well at 30-second intervals. Do not let the mixture boil as it could curdle. If necessary, reduce the power setting. When thickened, pour into warmed, sterilized jars and store in the refrigerator for two to four weeks.

See *Sterilizing*

CUSTARD

Make perfect custard every time in the microwave. Whisk together 2 tbsp custard powder, 2 tbsp sugar and 600 ml (1 pt) milk in a large jug. Microwave on 100% High for 2 minutes. Whisk well, microwave for a further 3–4 minutes on 50% Medium, whisking twice during cooking.

Increase the custard powder by 1 tbsp if a thicker custard is required to flavour and set in a mould or for a trifle.

CONFECTIONERS'–Crème Pâtissière

Confectioners' custard is a beautiful creamy filling used to sandwich puff pastries, choux pastries, sponges and as a base for fruit flans. It may also be used as a base for fruit fools. Quick and simple to make in the microwave.

Recipe 1 Blend 150 ml (¼ pt) milk with 1 tbsp castor sugar and 1 tbsp cornflour. Microwave on 100% High for 1½–2 minutes, stirring once during cooking. Add 1 egg yolk and a few drops of vanilla essence and beat well. Microwave on 100% High for 1–2 minutes until thick and creamy, whisking every 30 seconds. Do not allow it to boil. Remove from the cooker, cover to prevent a skin forming and leave to cool. Chill well before using to fill cakes and pastries. Add 15 g (½ oz) butter to the custard for a creamier filling.

Recipe 2 Blend 25 g (1 oz) flour, 25 g (1 oz) castor sugar with 1 egg. Microwave 150 ml (¼ pt) milk on 100% High for 1½–2 minutes. Pour over blended ingredients and whisk well. Microwave on 50% Medium for 1½–2 minutes until thick and creamy, whisking every 30 seconds. Do not allow it to boil. Flavour with a little vanilla essence. Cover, cool and use as above.

POURING EGG CUSTARD

Using a microwave for this recipe saves the bother of using double saucepans, and the custard is less likely to curdle.

Place 300 ml (½ pt) milk, 2 egg yolks and 25 g (1 oz) caster sugar in a bowl and whisk together. Microwave on 100% High for 3–4 minutes, whisking four times during cooking. Do not allow the custard to boil otherwise the eggs will curdle. If necessary, reduce the power setting. When cooked, the mixture should be thick enough to coat the back of a wooden spoon. Flavour with a few drops of vanilla essence.

D

DEFROSTING

When defrosting meat, unwrap then microwave on Low (Defrost). As a guide, 450 g (1lb) will take 5–10 minutes. Never completely defrost meat, poultry or fish in the microwave as the outside of the food will begin to dry out around the edges and may even start to cook. Remove when still cool and icy in the centre and leave to stand at room temperature to finish thawing.

When defrosting foods which have a high liquid content, e.g. sauces, soups, casseroles, etc., stir them as soon as possible, bringing the thawed edges into the centre and breaking into lumps when soft enough. If your microwave does not have a Low or Defrost control, heat on 100% High for 30 seconds then stand for at least 2 minutes. Repeat this process until the food is thawed, turning and repositioning the food each time it is heated.

As the variety of puddings, desserts and cakes is endless, it is difficult to advise on a power setting and timing. Refer to the manufacturer's instructions and if in doubt thaw them on Low or Defrost.

As a guide cover most foods with clingfilm, kitchen paper or place in a covered dish when thawing in a microwave.

DISHES

ARE THEY SAFE?

If in doubt as to whether a dish is microwave safe, put it in the cooker with a cup containing 150 ml (¼ pt) water. Microwave on 100% High for 1–2 minutes. If the dish remains cool to touch when the water is hot it is safe to use for microwave cooking.

BROWNING

It is important to follow the manufacturer's instructions when using a browning dish.

Browning dishes are versatile and produce a similar effect to grilling and frying. When food is placed on a hot browning dish, press it down using a spatula to give a better contact and increase the browning process. Do not cut food in the dish as it could damage the surface. Use oven gloves to remove the dish from the cooker as the underneath becomes very hot. Place a hot browning dish on a heatproof surface.

Use heat-resistant plastic or wooden utensils to turn and stir food on a browning dish or casserole.

CLAY

Glazed or not these dishes are excellent for microwave cookery, especially when cooking less tender cuts of meat. Soak the lid and dish in cold water for 10 minutes before use.

SIZE AND SHAPE

Use roughly the same principle when choosing size as for conventional cooking. If the food is likely to boil over, e.g. when heating milk, making chutneys, preserves, sauces, etc. make sure that the container is only half full before boiling point is reached.

High-sided dishes will shield the food being cooked so lessening the risk of sudden burning.

Shallow dishes hasten cooking time as the microwaves can reach the food more easily.

When possible choose dishes of an even shape with rounded corners if circular dishes are not suitable.

Food will also cook more evenly if the dish is given a half turn during cooking.

Ring-shaped dishes cook foods well if they cannot be stirred or turned. The microwaves are able to cook the food from the centre as well as from the outside, giving a more even and quicker result.

Stand a glass open end up in the middle of a round dish to make a ring dish for bread and cake making.

STRAW BASKETS

Straw baskets are useful for warming rolls, bread, teacakes, etc. because of the short cooking time required. Also the food may be warmed and served in the same dish, e.g. for use at a dinner party.

WOOD

As wood contains small amounts of moisture which evaporate during microwaving, dishes, bowls or boards should not be used in the microwave as they could crack.

DOUGH

See *Bread, Pizzas*

DUCK

Wash the duck inside and out and dry well. Tie legs and wings to form a neat shape and prick the skin all over to help release the fatty juices during cooking. Place an upturned saucer in a large dish and lay the duck on this breast side down. The fat and juice can then drain away easily. Alternatively, cook duck on a roasting rack. Cover loosely with greaseproof paper or an opened roasting bag to prevent spitting.

Microwave the duck on 100% High for 7–9 minutes per 450 g (1 lb). After one-quarter of the cooking time, drain the juices away and turn breast uppermost. Brush with a baste, glaze or browning agent and continue cooking, turning the dish and basting twice. Remove from the microwave, wrap in foil (shiny side inwards) and rest for 15 minutes. To test if the duck is cooked, insert a skewer through the thickest part of the leg. The flesh should be slightly pink and the juices clear.

Skim the fat from the drained juices and use the juices to enrich the flavour of an accompanying sauce.

STUFFED

If stuffing the cavity of a duck, weigh the bird after doing so to calculate the cooking time correctly.

See *Browning agents, Meat Glazes and Bastes*

DUMPLINGS

Dumplings can be cooked on top of a casserole or on their own. Add grated cheese, herbs and spices to the suet dough to give a variety of flavours. For a better appearance and flavour, brush dumplings with water and coat with savoury stuffing mixes.

To cook, place dumplings in a circle on a sheet of grease-proof paper and microwave on 100% High. Six average-sized dumplings will take 4–5 minutes. Leave to stand for 1 minute before serving.

E

EGGS

When cooking eggs conventionally the white sets before the yolk, but when cooked in the microwave the reverse happens and the yolk cooks first. The reason for this occurrence is that the yolk contains more fat than the white therefore attracting more microwave energy. If the egg is cooked until the white is set the yolk will be very hard. Because of this the standing time after microwaving is very important.

BAKED

Break two eggs into ramekin dishes or on a heated browning dish and prick the yolks with a cocktail stick. Cover with pierced clingfilm and microwave on 50% Medium for 2 minutes, turning dishes once during cooking. Leave to stand for 1–2 minutes. If using a browning dish reduce the cooking time by 20–30 seconds.

OMELETTE

Omelettes are quick to make when cooked in the microwave but will not brown in the dish. If cooking a plain omelette, lightly grease a 20 cm (8 inch) shallow dish with butter. Pour in the beaten egg mixture and microwave on 50% Medium for 3–4 minutes, turning the dish twice during cooking. Add meat and vegetables before or during cooking for a savoury omelette (calculating their cooking time accordingly).

Sweet omelettes can be made as above. Spread with warmed jam or fill with fruit after cooking. Fold in half and sprinkle with icing sugar.

To make a puffy, light omelette, separate four eggs. Beat the yolks with 2 tbsp milk and a pinch of sugar or seasonings (for sweet or savoury). Whisk egg whites until stiff and fold into the yolk mixture. Microwave on 50% Medium for 5–7 minutes until the centre is set.

PIERCING

When microwaving a whole broken egg always pierce the yolk at least once with a cocktail stick to break the membrane. Failure to do this will result in the egg exploding during cooking.

POACHED

Place 2 tbsp water and ¼ tsp vinegar into a ramekin dish. Cover and microwave on 100% High for 30–40 seconds or until boiling. Break an egg into the dish and pierce yolk. Cover with pierced clingfilm and microwave on 50% Medium for 15–30 seconds. Stand for 1 minute before serving. For more than one egg turn the dishes halfway through cooking time and adjust the timing accordingly.

SCRAMBLED

Scrambled eggs cooked in the microwave are fluffier and have more volume than if conventionally cooked. Place 15 g (½ oz) butter in a bowl and microwave on 100% High for a few seconds until melted. Beat in two eggs and 2 tbsp milk. Microwave on 100% High for 2–2¼ minutes, stirring with a fork halfway through cooking time. Season, mix thoroughly, cover and leave to stand for 1½ minutes as the mixture will continue to cook.

Butter in the recipe may be omitted for the calorie conscious as it is only used for flavour. Also the milk may be replaced by water. The result is a less creamy mixture.

TEMPERATURE

To bring a refrigerated egg to room temperature, microwave on 100% High for 5 seconds. Do not microwave for longer as it may explode. If you do not have a digital timer on your microwave cooker, check the timing by using the second hand of a watch, timer or clock.

WHITE

An egg white at room temperature will whisk to a much greater volume than one that has been refrigerated.

YOLK

Refrigerated eggs are more likely to curdle when mixed with butter or oil. Bring them to room temperature by beating 2 yolks in a bowl and microwave on 100% High for 10 seconds. This should then prevent them from curdling.

F

FAT

Clarify fat after roasting or boiling meats by placing it in a bowl with a little water. Microwave on 100% High until it starts to boil, strain and leave to set. The sediment will fall to the bottom and the clarified fat can be removed from the top. Place this in a clean bowl, melt on Low (Defrost) and pour into a clean container. Cool, cover and keep in the refrigerator for up to four weeks.

FISH

Microwaved fish retains its delicate flavour and unlike meat does not need browning to appeal to the eye. The appearance of cooked fish can be transformed with the addition of garnishes, sauces and flavoured butters.

The microwave is an excellent method of cooking fish as all the moisture and odours are retained in the covered dish. Only microwave until the fish starts to flake, then stand for 2 minutes to ensure the centre or thicker part is thoroughly cooked.

Always score the skin on fish two or three times before cooking and remove the eyes if cooked whole, or they will burst.

CAKES AND FINGERS

These can be cooked in the microwave without being defrosted.

Melt a little butter or margarine and brush the fingers or cakes on both sides. Lay six on a prepared browning dish or buttered plate and microwave on 100% High for 3 minutes, rearranging two or three times during cooking and turning over once. (The use of a browning dish will produce better results.)

HERRINGS – Pickled (Rollmops)

Remove the heads and tails of four cleaned herrings. Fillet and roll up, skin side out, securing each one with a wooden cocktail stick. Place a single layer in a dish and sprinkle with 1 onion, finely sliced, 2 tsp sugar, 10 whole peppercorns, 4 bay leaves, 2 tsp pickling spice, 300 ml (½ pt) cider vinegar.

Cover and microwave for 8–10 minutes, rearranging herrings halfway through cooking time. Uncover and cool the herrings in the juices.

Chill in the refrigerator before serving as a starter or with salads.

KIPPERS

Frozen bagged kippers are easily microwaved, retaining most of their odours. To cook a small bag from frozen, pierce and put on a plate. Microwave on 100% High for 4 minutes and leave to stand for 2 minutes to finish cooking before serving.

POACHING

Poached fish is cooked in a small amount of liquid (e.g. lemon juice, water, milk, fish stock, white wine). Unlike meat this may be seasoned with salt and poured over the fish without any danger of toughening or drying it out.

Lay 450 g (1lb) fish fillets, cutlets or steaks in a dish, add liquid, cover and microwave on 100% High for 4–6 minutes. Thicker fleshed fish, e.g. cod, will take at least 6 minutes as will stuffed fillets. Whole fish will take 5–7 minutes. Stand for 2–3 minutes before serving.

ROE

Soft roe cooks beautifully in the microwave. As no liquid is needed to cook them, their true flavour can be appreciated. Prick 225 g (8 oz) of roes a few times to break the membrane and place a single layer in a buttered dish. Cover and microwave on 100% High for 2 minutes. Turn and rearrange the roes and cook for a further 2 minutes. Season with black pepper and stand for 2 minutes before serving. Roes are a lovely snack served on toast, topped with lemon sauce and sprinkled with chopped parsley.

TROUT

Clean and prepare the fish, season inside and arrange on a shallow dish, head to tail. Dot with butter and sprinkle over a little lemon juice. Cover with a lid and microwave on 100% High until the fish just begins to flake. Stand for 2–3 minutes before serving. Trout may be stuffed, if preferred. Weigh the fish and microwave for 4 minutes per 450 g (1 lb) in either case.

Serve with a sprinkling of toasted almonds or a small carton of soured cream mixed with 1 tsp chopped parsley. Warm for 45–60 seconds on 100% High. Pour over the trout and garnish with watercress and lemon slices.

WHOLE BREADED

Use the same method as for fish fingers. Two portions of breaded plaice will take 4–5 minutes from frozen, rearranging and turning over once during cooking.

See *Butter, Flavoured, Stocks* and *Sauces*

FLAMBÉEING

Warm brandy, etc. in the microwave when required for flambéed foods.

However, heating spirits of any kind in a microwave carries an element of risk if left unattended. The spirit should only be allowed to warm but not reach anywhere near boiling point otherwise it could ignite. About 2 tbsp spirit or liqueur will take no longer than 15–20 seconds on 100% High. For safety, measure the amount of spirit required and pour into a heat-proof container and warm. Do not use a wine glass.

FLOUR

When bread making, warm flour for 15 seconds on 100% High to assist in proving and rising dough.

FOIL

Most manufacturers state that small pieces of foil can be used in the microwave provided that certain safety measures are adhered to. Refer to your personal handbook for their specific instructions.

Foil is a good conductor of heat and is used mainly for keeping food hot and to complete its cooking during the standing time. Wrap food in foil with the shiny side in to reflect the heat back into the food.

FONDUE

Do not try to keep fondues constantly hot in the microwave as they can curdle with excessive prolonged heating. As soon as the ingredients are melted, blended and hot, pour into a fondue warmer and serve. Microwaved fondues tend to be a little thinner in consistency than when conventionally cooked, so thicken with a little cornflour or increase the quantity slightly in the recipe.

FRUIT

DRIED

Dried fruit may be swollen to full capacity in the microwave without soaking beforehand. Put 125 g (4 oz) dried fruit (e.g. raisins, mixed fruit, sultanas, etc.) in a shallow dish and sprinkle with 3 tbsp water. Cover with pierced clingfilm and microwave on 100% High for 3 minutes until soft. Stir two or three times during cooking. Leave to stand for 3 minutes, cool and drain before using.

Alcohol may be used instead of water: use 4 tbsp. Stir several times during cooking otherwise spot burning may occur because of the high concentration of sugar.

When cooking larger fruits (e.g. apricots, figs, pears, peaches) a better result will be obtained if they are soaked overnight in cold water, then drained and cooked as above.

EXTRACTING JUICE

See *Citrus, Fruits*

PEELING

Depending on the size of individual fruits, the timing given for peeling can vary considerably. Microwave larger fruit, such as peaches, for 15–20 seconds, microwave two smaller fruits, like apricots, for 15–20 seconds. Stand for 1 minute before removing the skin.

POACHING

Poach fruit whole with sugar syrup when serving as a dessert, to increase their succulence, taste and appearance. As a general guide to poaching fresh fruit, prick the skins if cooking whole so that they do not burst. Place 450 g (1 lb) in a dish with 300 ml (½ pt) sugar syrup, cover with pierced clingfilm and microwave on 100% High for 3–6 minutes. Stir once during cooking.

When poaching fruit to soften for use in flans, pies or for the calorie conscious, place in a bowl with 1 tbsp water, cover with pierced clingfilm and microwave on 100% High for 3–4 minutes. Stir once during cooking if the fruit is halved and stoned. Stand for 2–3 minutes before serving.

If wished, stone the fruit and reduce with 150 ml (¼ pt) of syrup to a purée in a liquidizer or food processor. Use as a sauce for ice-cream, sponge puddings, etc. or add to confectioners' custard to make a rich fruit fool.

Greengages and plums can be microwaved without using sugar syrup or additional water as they are very juicy. They hold their shape well and make a good filling for flan cases. Halve and stone 450 g (1 lb) fruit and arrange cut side down in a dish. Cover and microwave on 100% High for 2–3 minutes, rearranging and turning the dish once during cooking. Cool and use as required.

BERRY FRUITS

Prick the skins and microwave as above for 1–3 minutes if poaching, 3–5 minutes if puréeing. If puréeing, only use 2 tbsp sugar syrup otherwise it will be watery. Sweeten the purée with sugar if it is too tart.

GLACÉ FRUITS

Glacé fruits can be made by preparing a caramel syrup in the microwave. Choose fresh strawberries, orange segments, grapes, pineapple pieces OR tinned peaches, apricots, maraschino cherries, provided the fruit is drained and dried beforehand.

Lightly brush a dish or plate with oil. Place 125 g (4 oz) sugar and 5 tbsp hot water in a deep jug. Microwave uncovered on 100% High for 1½–2 minutes until the sugar has dissolved. Stir once during cooking. Add 1 tsp glucose powder, stir well and microwave on 100% High for 5–6 minutes until it just starts to turn brown. Check the syrup frequently for this.

Place the jug of syrup on a wet cloth to reduce the temperature or add 1 tsp water. As soon as it stops boiling, spear the fruits on cocktail sticks and dip in the syrup. Shake off excess syrup and leave to set on the prepared dish. When cool and crisp place in paper cases.

See *Sugar Syrup*

G

GAME

Game cooks best on a 50% Medium setting. Use a browning agent to coat the skin if a deeper colour is preferred or cook in a roasting bag. This will also keep the meat moist and assist in browning it.

As a guide, microwave game on 50% Medium for 8–10 minutes per 450 g (lb). Use the same setting and timing if casseroling.

Do not overcook game as the flesh becomes dry and very tough.

RABBIT

Follow the same basic rules as microwaving chicken. Rabbit cooks particularly well in a casserole.

See *Chicken*

GARNISHES

Microwave cookery is a moist form of heat, which softens ingredients, but does not brown them.

Try to use crisp garnishes whenever possible to give more 'bite' to a food and improve its appearance.

Sprinkle vegetables and sauces with: crushed crisps, browned breadcrumbs, nuts, crushed crackers and cornflakes, crisp fried bacon pieces, cheese, crushed dried onion rings.

GELATINE

To dissolve gelatine, place 3 tbsp water in a bowl and sprinkle over 1 level tbsp gelatine. Leave for a couple of minutes until firm then microwave on 100% High for 1 minute until gelatine is dissolved. Stir well before using.

GOOSEBERRIES

See *Fruit*

GLAZES

See *Butter, Flavoured* and *Meat Glazes and Bastes*

GRAPEFRUIT

To 'grill' a grapefruit in the microwave, halve, loosen the segments and place in a dish. Pour over 1 tbsp rum or sherry and sprinkle with 2 tsp brown sugar. Microwave on 100% High for 1 minute. Top with a maraschino cherry and serve as a quick starter.

See *Citrus, Curds*

GRAPES

FROSTING

Break a bunch of grapes into stems of two or three and dip into 1 egg white, lightly beaten, tapping off any excess liquid. Dip into castor sugar, coating generously and taking care not to sugar stalks. Place a piece of greaseproof paper on the base of the cooker and arrange the grapes in a circle. Microwave on Low (Defrost) for approximately 3 minutes, turning over halfway through cooking time. The sugar casing should be dry and crisp to the touch. Use frosted grapes to decorate special desserts, e.g. soufflés, flans, pavlovas.

GRAVY

To make a quick and simple gravy, place 2 tsp meat dripping, 1 tbsp plain flour and 300 ml (½ pt) meat juices/stock in a jug. Whisk well and microwave on 100% High for 2–3 minutes, whisking twice during cooking. Season with salt and pepper. Darken the gravy with a little browning if a richer colour is preferred.

GREENGAGES

See *Fruit, Poaching*

GREASEPROOF PAPER

See *Covering Food*

H

HAZELNUTS

To roast and skin hazelnuts, put 50 g (2 oz) shelled nuts in a dish and microwave on 100% High for 2–2½ minutes, tossing two or three times during cooking. Cool and rub nuts between hands to remove skins.

HERBS

DRYING

Wash and dry well. Spread a layer on a sheet of kitchen paper and place on the base of the cooker with a cup of water. Cover with another sheet of paper and microwave on 100% High until the herbs dull in colour and crumble easily. Rearrange several times during cooking and check for dryness at 30-second intervals. Leave to cool, crumble and store in an airtight jar in a cool dark place.

See *Seasonings*

HONEY

To melt honey which has crystallized, heat on 50% Medium or Low (Defrost) for 20–60 seconds, removing the metal lid before placing jar in the microwave.

I

ICE CREAM

MAKING

Ice-creams are easily made in the microwave using an egg custard base.

Place 300 ml (½ pt) milk and 125 g (4 oz) castor sugar in a bowl. Microwave on 100% High for 2–2½ minutes, stirring once during cooking. The milk should not boil, but be warm enough to dissolve the sugar. Whisk in 2 beaten eggs and 1 tsp vanilla essence and microwave on 100% High for 2–3 minutes, whisking twice during cooking. The custard should thicken and be smooth. Cool and fold in 300 ml (½ pt) whipped double cream. Pour into a container, cover and leave until just starting to set around the edge. Whisk well, return to the freezer and leave to re-set.

Adjust this basic recipe to create a variety of ice-creams. Omit the vanilla essence and flavour the custard with almond, fruit or coffee essence.

Add chocolate chips, chopped glacé fruits, dried fruit and nuts to give texture.

Add a few drops of food colouring if desired.

Serve the ice-cream with fresh or tinned fruit, wafer biscuits or meringues and top with a sauce.

See *Cakes, Fillings and Toppings* and *Sauces*

SOFTENING

Ice-cream can be softened in the microwave so that it is pliable enough to make bombes or set in moulds. Place 1 litre (1¾ pt) block of ice-cream in a bowl and microwave on Low (Defrost) for 1½–2 minutes. Chill moulds in the freezer before adding the ice-cream.

UNMOULDING

To loosen ice-cream from a mould or a container (not metal), microwave on Low (Defrost) for 15–30 seconds.

ICING

FONDANT

To make fondant icing more pliable and easier to use, wrap 225 g (8 oz) fondant in clingfilm and microwave on Low (Defrost) for 1–1½ minutes.

To melt fondant icing, place 225 g (8 oz) in a bowl and microwave on 100% High for 1½–2 minutes, stirring twice during cooking. Flavour or colour the icing if preferred. The icing will set on cooling.

Use to ice sponges or half dip fresh fruit, e.g. strawberries (leave hulls on), into the icing, then into chopped nuts. Leave to set. Serve as an after-dinner sweet.

ROYAL

Royal icing flowers and lattice patterns can be dried in the microwave on a Low (Defrost) or 10% setting. Do not microwave for longer than 15 seconds and leave to stand for 4-minute intervals.

INSULATING DISHES AND FOOD

Food cooked for a short time in the microwave cools quickly during standing time because the dish does not get hot and therefore cannot transfer heat to the food. Insulate dishes to assist in retaining heat in the food by placing them in a quilted holder, basket or by wrapping in napkins. They will also look more attractive on the table when serving.

To keep food hot during the standing time and to finish off the cooking process, cover or wrap in foil, shiny side in, so that the heat is reflected back into the food.

J

JAM

COOKING

Microwaved jam eliminates any condensation, odours and splattering.

Sugar added to the fruit must be dissolved before the jam has started to boil. To help this process, warm 450 g (1 lb) sugar on 50% Medium for 2 minutes. Use a 2.8 litre (5 pt) bowl for up to 1 kg (2 lb) fruit and stir regularly during the cooking time. A general rule is to use a container at least three times as large as the amount of ingredients being used.

QUANTITY

Do not make more than 1.8 kg (4 lb) jam at one time.

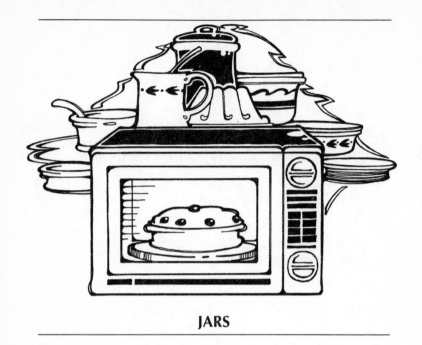

JARS

See *Sterilizing*

JELLY

DISSOLVING

Cut a packet of jelly into pieces or pull cubes apart. Place in a jug or bowl with 300 ml (½ pt) water. Microwave on 100% High for 1½–2 minutes, stirring once during cooking. Remove from the cooker and stir until the jelly has dissolved. Make up to 600 ml (1 pt) with ice-cubes and cold water. The jelly will then set in much less time.

UNMOULDING

To loosen made-up jellies from their moulds, microwave on Low (Defrost) for 30 seconds.

K

KEBABS

Always use wooden skewers and marinate the fish or meat kebabs for 2 hours to give more flavour, colour and tenderness to the food. Place four kebabs on a plate or prepared browning dish and brush with remaining marinade or a sauce of your choice. Cover with kitchen paper or greaseproof and microwave on 100% High for 3–4 minutes, then on Low (Defrost) for 10–12 minutes. Turn the kebabs regularly and baste with marinade during cooking.

Kebabs can also be microwaved on 50% Medium for 12–14 minutes if your cooker has a variable control.

Fish Kebabs can be cooked on 100% High for 4–6 minutes.

See *Marinades*

Remove the membrane encasing the kidney, cut in half and snip out the core using scissors. Kidneys can also be 'fried' like liver, using a browning dish. 450 g (1 lb) lamb's kidneys will take 8–10 minutes on 100% High. Turn and rearrange during cooking. Pig's and ox kidneys are tougher than lamb's, so require a lower power setting and longer cooking time.

KIDNEY BEANS

Do not attempt to cook kidney beans in the microwave as they should be boiled at a constant temperature by the conventional method to make them safe enough to eat.

KITCHEN PAPER

See *Covering Food*

L

LEEKS

Leeks cook well in a microwave. As so little water is used they keep their shape, colour and flavour well. Choose leeks of a uniform size so that they cook evenly. Trim the roots and tops of 450 g (1 lb) leeks, wash and place a single layer in a dish. Sprinkle with 4 tbsp water, cover and microwave on 100% High for 4–6 minutes, rearranging once during cooking. Stand for 3 minutes, drain and serve with white or cheese sauce.

See *Sauces*

LEMONS

See *Citrus, Curds*

LIMES

See *Citrus, Curds*

LIQUEURS

See *Wines and Liqueurs in Drinks*

LIQUIDS

Liquids should be heated in large, wide-necked jugs rather than tall, narrow jugs to reduce the risk of them boiling over.

Use conventional means when heating 600 ml (1 pt) or more of liquid as it will warm faster than using the microwave. This is important when adding stock, etc. to casseroles and soups as it will affect the cooking time.

LIVER

Liver cooks quickly and evenly in the microwave. There is less shrinkage and the meat remains moist. However, overcooking will toughen it, so timing is important. When cooked, the meat should be just pink when cut.

Slice the liver or prick with a fork to break the membrane. It can be 'fried' in the microwave using a browning dish. Cover with kitchen paper or greaseproof to prevent spitting. 450 g (1 lb) liver will take 6–8 minutes on 100% High. Reduce the timing by 2 minutes if using calf's liver as it has a more delicate texture.

LOW FAT SPREADS

Low fat spreads usually separate when used in conventional cookery but this does not happen when heated in the microwave. They are ideal to use as a glaze for food if you are calorie conscious. Use as a substitute for butter in flavoured butter, halving the microwave time when heating.

See *Butter, Flavoured*

M

MARGARINE

See *Butter*

MARINADES

Steep meat overnight or for a few hours in a marinade, if possible. It will add extra flavour, tenderize the meat and assist in browning, so making it more appealing.

Use marinades for steaks, chops, cutlets, chicken portions: generally any meats that are usually grilled.

Drain the meat and use the remaining marinade as a baste during cooking or thicken with cornflour and serve as an accompanying sauce.

BASIC

Combine equal quantities of vegetable oil and lemon juice. Add spices or herbs from the following: crushed black peppercorns, onion powder, crushed garlic cloves or powder, barbecue seasoning, lamb, pork or chicken seasoning, fresh or dried herbs, mustard, tomato sauce, Worcestershire sauce, soy sauce, ginger, sugar, vinegar etc.

BARBECUE

Mix 4 tbsp tomato sauce, 4 tbsp brown sauce, 2 tbsp Worcestershire sauce, 2 tbsp soft brown sugar, 1 tsp mustard. Use for chicken and pork.

LEMON

Mix 3 tbsp oil, 3 tbsp lemon juice, ½ tsp black pepper, 1 tbsp chopped fresh parsley. Use for fish.

WINE

Mix 150 ml (¼ pt) dry red wine, 3 tbsp oil, 3 tbsp red wine vinegar, 1 tsp thyme, 1 tbsp brown sugar. Use for lamb and beef.

MARMALADE

Cook marmalades in the microwave using the same basic principles of jam but remember the peel of citrus fruit takes longer to soften than jam-making fruit. To assist the softening, place chopped or shredded peel in a bowl with 150 ml (¼ pt) water. Cover and microwave on 100% High for 5–7 minutes. The softened peel may then be added to the other ingredients. Chop the pips and tie in a muslin bag to help release the pectin during microwaving. Remove when setting point is reached.

See *Jam*

MARROW

DICE

Marrow can be cooked in slices or dice without the addition of any water.

Place 450 g (1 lb) diced marrow in a dish. Cover and microwave on 100% for 6–8 minutes, tossing twice during cooking. Season and leave to stand for 2 minutes. Serve with a mild mustard or cheese sauce.

STUFFED

Place stuffed rings of sliced marrow in a casserole with 4 tbsp stock. Cover with pierced clingfilm and microwave on 100% High for 6–8 minutes. Rearrange the rings, turn the dish and baste once during cooking. Leave to stand for 2 minutes before serving with tomato sauce.

See *Sauce, Tomato*

MARZIPAN

To make marzipan more pliable and easier to use, wrap 225 g (8 oz) in clingfilm and microwave on Low (Defrost) for 1–1½ minutes.

MEAT

As a general rule, if the total cooking time is 15 minutes or more, a joint brushed with unsalted butter will brown naturally. It is best, however, to assist this process by brushing meat with a browning agent or glaze before microwaving. Seal meat under a grill or in a frying pan or cook in a roasting bag.

Cook joints of meat on an upturned saucer in a dish so juices can drain away. Do not add or sprinkle meat with salt before or during cooking as it dries it out (the exception being the crackling on pork).

Leave meat covered and at room temperature for 30–60 minutes before microwaving. Turn joints of meat frequently during cooking and leave to stand wrapped in foil, shiny side inwards, for 15–30 minutes before carving.

Place thicker parts of chops, etc. towards the outside of the dish, turn over and rotate the dish during cooking. When reheating sliced meat, add 1 tbsp stock or thin gravy per portion to help keep it moist and succulent.

See *Browning Agents, Casseroles, Chicken, Coatings, Duck, Meat Glazes and Bastes, Turkey*

BASIC COOKING GUIDES FOR JOINTS

Baste joints of meat except pork during microwaving, unless cooking in a roasting bag. Timings are for 100% High or 50% Medium settings per 450 g (1 lb).

BEEF

	Minutes at 100% High	Minutes at 50% Medium	
TOPSIDE	5	10–11	rare
	6–7	11–13	medium
	8–9	14–16	well done
RIB	7	13–15	rare
	8–9	14–16	medium
	9–12	16–18	well done
RIB	6	11–12	rare
BONED and	7–8	13–15	medium
ROLLED	9–10	16–18	well done
SIRLOIN	5	10–11	rare
	6–7	11–13	medium
	8–9	14–16	well done

LAMB

LEG	8–9	10–12
BONED AND ROLLED	9–10	13–14
SHOULDER	9–10	13–14

PORK

Do not cover. Oil the skin and rub in salt. Leg and loin joints with the bone in should be microwaved on 100% High for the first 8 minutes, then on 50% Medium for 17–18 minutes per 450 g (1 lb).

Shoulder joints with the bone in – microwave on 100% High for the first 8 minutes, then on 50% Medium for 14–16 minutes per 450 g (1 lb).

BACON, GAMMON AND HAM JOINTS

Cook these joints in a roasting bag and follow the same basic rules as for cooking meat. It is best to cook bacon joints on a 50% Medium setting for 10–16 minutes per 450 g (1 lb), depending on the tenderness of the cut.

Wrap cooked joints in foil after microwaving and stand for 15–30 minutes to finish the cooking.

It is safest to use a temperature probe to test if joints of meat are cooked.

See *Temperature Probe*

MEAT GLAZES AND BASTES

Whenever possible, use unsalted butter in a baste as salt will toughen the food.

FOR BACON, GAMMON AND HAM

1. 3 tbsp clear honey mixed with the rind and juice of 1 orange and 1 tbsp soft brown sugar.
2. 1 small jar of cranberry jelly mixed with 4 tbsp cider vinegar.

FOR BEEF

Microwaved beef browns quite well without the assistance of a glaze. Use the drained meat juices to enhance a gravy or sauce.

FOR CHICKEN

1. 4 tbsp clear honey mixed with 1 tbsp sherry.

2. Grated rind and juice of 1 lemon mixed with 1 tsp mustard and 1 tbsp brown sauce.

3. 4 tbsp tomato ketchup mixed with 2 tbsp brown sugar, 1 tsp mustard, 1 tsp Worcestershire sauce, 1 tbsp cider vinegar.

FOR DUCK

1. 4 tbsp marmalade mixed with 4 tbsp dry white wine.

2. 4 tbsp cranberry sauce or jelly mixed with 1 tbsp lemon juice and 3 tbsp dry red wine.

3. 4 tbsp apricot, peach, cherry or pineapple purée mixed with 2 tbsp sherry or port and 1 tbsp lemon juice.

FOR LAMB

1. 2 tbsp marmalade mixed with 2 tbsp clear honey, 2 tsp lemon juice, 2 tsp Worcestershire sauce.

2. 4 tbsp mint jelly mixed with 2 tbsp red wine vinegar, 2 tsp brown sugar.

3. 4 tbsp redcurrant jelly mixed with 3 tbsp sherry and 1 tbsp lemon juice.

FOR PORK

1. 4 tbsp clear honey mixed with 1 tbsp dry cider and 1 tsp chopped sage.

2. 4 tbsp barbecue sauce mixed with 1 tbsp clear honey and 1 tsp soy sauce.

3. 2 tbsp clear honey mixed with 4 tbsp dry cider and 1 tsp dried sage.

MERINGUES

Crisp, white meringues can be cooked in minutes in the microwave. Whisk one egg white until frothy and gradually mix in 350 g (12 oz) sifted icing sugar. When the mixture stiffens, knead by hand to form a ball. Divide in two and roll each piece into a long sausage. Cut both lengths into 24 pieces, roll these into balls and place 6 in a ring on a sheet of greaseproof paper. Microwave on 100% High for 1½–2 minutes until well risen, crisp and dry. Leave to stand for 5 minutes, remove paper and cool on a rack. Repeat with the remaining 42 pieces.

Store cooked meringues in an airtight container for up to three weeks.

The meringue mixture may be coloured if preferred and when cooked sandwiched together with fresh cream or dipped in chocolate. Knead 50 g (2 oz) desiccated coconut into the sugar dough for coconut meringues.

Conventional recipe meringue toppings can be microwaved (e.g. lemon meringue pie) but the result will be soft and white. Microwave on 100% High for 1½–2 minutes. Brown under a hot grill or sprinkle with coconut or brown sugar before microwaving. Decorate with cherries and angelica.

PAVLOVA

Roll half of the meringue mixture to a 16–18 cm (6–7 inch) circle on a sheet of greaseproof paper. Microwave on 100% High for 1½–2 minutes. When cold, decorate with fruit and cream.

MILK

Heat milk for cereals in a bowl by microwaving 150 ml (¼ pt) on 100% High for 20–30 seconds.

A cup or mug of hot milk will take 1½–2 minutes on 100% High.

See *Puddings, Milk*

MOISTURE

Whenever possible wrap moist and starchy foods in clingfilm to prevent evaporation, e.g. reheating jacket potatoes, corn on the cob, sweet or savoury puddings.

MOUSSE

To loosen mousses from their moulds microwave on Low (Defrost) for 30 seconds.

MUSHROOMS

Try to choose mushrooms of a uniform size so that they will cook evenly. Wash, pat dry and trim the stems. Do not peel the skins. Place 125 g (4 oz) mushrooms in a dish with 15 g (½ oz) butter and a squeeze of lemon juice. Cover and microwave on 100% High for 2–3 minutes, stirring halfway through cooking time. Stand for 1 minute before serving. Use any juices to flavour stocks, sauces and gravies.

STUFFED

To microwave 225 g (8 oz) stuffed mushrooms, wash, pat dry and remove stalks. Mound your favourite filling into the mushroom cap and arrange them on a plate lined with a sheet of kitchen paper. Microwave on 100% High for 3–4 minutes. Flat or large cap mushrooms are the best choice as the cavity is much larger than button.

MUSSELS

See *Shellfish*

N

NECTARINES

See *Fruit*

NUTS

ENHANCING FLAVOUR

Place 225 g (8 oz) salted peanuts in a dish and microwave on 100% High for 20–30 seconds.

REFRESHING

To re-crisp soft shelled nuts, heat on 100% High for ½–1 minute.

To re-crisp unshelled, plain roasted peanuts (monkey nuts), put 125 g (4 oz) nuts in a dish and place in the microwave. Cook uncovered on 100% High for 1½–2 minutes, tossing two or three times during cooking. Cool and shell.

ROASTING AND SALTING

Place 175 g (6 oz) shelled and husked nuts in a shallow dish with 1 tsp oil. Microwave on 100% High for 3–5 minutes or until lightly browned, tossing every minute. Lay on kitchen paper and cool. If salting, sprinkle over nuts and toss while still warm.

SHELLING

To make shelling easier, place 225 g (8 oz) Brazils, almonds, pecans, walnuts, hazelnuts (or an assortment) in a large bowl and pour over 225 ml (8 fl oz) water. Cover and microwave on 100% High for 3–4 minutes or until water boils. Stand for 1 minute, drain and spread on kitchen paper to cool. The nuts may then be cracked open, taking care because the shells may contain hot water.

SPICED

Mix 225 g (8 oz) peanuts with 1 tsp spice of your choice, e.g. curry, Worcestershire sauce, chilli, garlic, etc., and 15 g (½ oz) melted butter. Mix well and microwave uncovered on 100% High for 1½–2½ minutes, tossing two or three times during cooking. These are best served warm to enjoy their full flavour.

See *Almonds, Chestnuts, Hazelnuts*

O

ODOURS

Occasionally the microwave may need to be refreshed if strong smelling foods have been cooked, e.g. kippers or chutneys. Place 2 slices of lemon in a jug of hot water and microwave on 100% High for 2 minutes.

Remove the jug and wipe the inside of the cooker with a clean dry cloth.

ONIONS

Peel 450 g (1 lb) medium-sized onions. Place in a casserole, cover and microwave on 100% High for 8–10 minutes, re-arranging and turning the dish once during cooking. Sprinkle with salt and leave to stand for 2 minutes. Serve with a sour cream dressing or white sauce.

STUFFED

Stuffed onions can be cooked as above. Scoop out the centre and fill with stuffing. Add 4 tbsp stock and cover with pierced clingfilm. Baste the onions with stock twice during cooking. Leave to stand for 2 minutes before serving. Serve with tomato sauce.

See *Sauces*

ORANGES

See *Citrus, Curds*

P

PANCAKES

Batters cannot be cooked in the microwave. However, pancakes can be reheated. Loosely roll four cooked pancakes and arrange on a plate. Cover with clingfilm and microwave on 100% High for 40–60 seconds.

PARSNIPS

When microwaving parsnips add 1 tbsp lemon juice to the water before cooking to retain their white colour.

Prepare 450 g (1 lb) parsnips, turnips or swedes (or a combination) and place in a dish with 3 tbsp water. Cover and microwave on 100% High for 9–12 minutes, tossing twice during cooking. Stand for 3 minutes.

Season, drain and serve with cheese or lemon sauce. Swedes are best diced, cooked and mashed with a little butter and sprinkled with nutmeg.

DRIED

Place 225 g (8 oz) pasta in a deep dish and cover with boiling water, adding 1 tsp salt and 1 tbsp oil. Stir well and without covering microwave on 100% High for 5–6 minutes, stirring twice during cooking to prevent the pasta from sticking together. Stand covered for 5 minutes, then drain and serve for perfect pasta.

FRESH

Place 225 g (8 oz) fresh pasta in a deep dish. Cover with salted boiling water and microwave on 100% High for 2–3 minutes. Stir once during cooking.

PRE-COOKED PASTA

Cannelloni and lasagne that does not require pre-cooking can be used in your favourite recipe and microwaved successfully. Make the meat fillings more moist and increase the quantity of sauce slightly to give a thicker coating to the pasta. Only sprinkle the top of the food with cheese 2 minutes before the end of the cooking time otherwise it will be tough and stringy. A recipe using 8–10 cannelloni will take 8–10 minutes on 100% High. Brown under a hot grill or garnish with sliced tomato and sprinkle with chopped parsley. Use the same method for lasagne. Serve with garlic or herb French bread.

See *Bread, French*

PASTRY

COOKING

After cooking a pastry case, seal the pricked base by brushing with beaten egg yolk. Microwave on 100% High for 30–60 seconds or until yolk has set. This will prevent any filling, such as fruit and lemon meringue, seeping through to the pastry and making it soggy.

PASTRY SHAPES

Roll out any pastry trimmings and cut into small shapes to decorate desserts or serve with soups and casseroles. Microwave as for 'lids', adjusting the cooking time to suit the amount to be microwaved.

PUFF

Puff pastry cooks well in the microwave but watch it carefully as the inside browns while the outside is still pale. After rolling out, chill the pastry in the refrigerator for 30 minutes before cooking. When the pastry is cooked it should hold its shape and not flop when the oven door is opened. Lay a rectangle of rolled and prepared pastry on two sheets of kitchen paper and microwave on 100% High. 125 g (4 oz) will take 2–3 minutes.

SHORTCRUST BASES

Do not attempt to cook double-crust pies or filled flan cases in the microwave. The filling will cook before the pastry, making it wet and doughy.

Shortcrust pastry bases cook well on their own if a few basic rules are followed:

1. Do not add sugar to the pastry before cooking as it will burn.

2. Chill the pastry base in the refrigerator for 30 minutes before microwaving.

3. Use a mixture of brown and white flour to make the pastry.

4. Add a few drops of yellow food colouring to the mixture to improve the appearance.

5. Prick the base and sides of the pastry case well before cooking.

6. Line the base of the pastry case with two sheets of kitchen paper for the first half of the cooking time, to absorb moisture.

7. Do not attempt to cook a base larger than 23 cm (9 inch) in diameter.

8. Place the prepared flan dish on an upturned saucer in the microwave to assist in even cooking.

A 20–23 cm (8–9 inch) pastry base will take 4–5 minutes to cook on 100% High. Turn the dish every minute.

SHORTCRUST LIDS

To make a 'false' lid for a pie, roll pastry to 20 cm (8 inch) circle, prick well and chill. Place on a sheet of non-stick paper (not waxed) in the cooker and microwave on 100% High for 2–3 minutes until crisp and dry. Mark the pastry into sections before cooking if desired so that it can be portioned easily.

A dusting of paprika, microwave seasoning or sesame seeds before microwaving will improve the colour when cooked.

SHORTCRUST TARTLETS

Follow the same rules for pastry bases. Either use special microwave tartlet trays or mould small circles of pastry round upturned dishes or ramekins.

SUET

Suet pastry cannot be 'baked' using a microwave. It is only suitable for use in pudding and dumpling recipes, producing excellent results and reducing the cooking time to minutes.

See *Dumplings and Puddings*

REHEATING PIES

Cover pies loosely with kitchen paper to help retain a crisp pastry.

Sweet pie fillings become extremely hot when reheated due to the high sugar content, but the pastry remains cool. Leave them to stand after microwaving to equalize the temperature.

PÂTÉ

Pâtés cook beautifully in the microwave and the cooking time is considerably shorter than the conventional method. Most conventional recipes can be converted for the microwave, although the finished result may be slightly wetter than usual. Reduce the liquid content slightly in the recipe and adjust the seasonings, because they intensify with microwave cookery.

Try to cook pâtés in round dishes rather than oblong so that they cook more evenly. As a general rule, pâté using 450 g (1 lb) of pig's liver will take 7–10 minutes on 100% High. Cover the top of the pâté with greaseproof paper during cooking.

SOFTENING

To soften stiff pâtés for easier spreading, remove foil wrappings. Cover with clingfilm and microwave on Low (Defrost) for a few seconds.

PAVLOVA

See *Meringue*

PEACHES

See *Fruit*

PEARS

As pears discolour once peeled, brush with lemon juice before poaching in sugar syrup or poach in a red wine sugar syrup.

Place four peeled and cored pears in a deep dish and pour over sugar syrup, coating them well. Cover and microwave on 100% High for 5–7 minutes, turning the dish halfway through cooking. Stand for 3 minutes. Serve hot with cream or custard or leave to cool, turning the pears in the syrup at intervals to flavour and colour them evenly. Serve chilled with fresh cream.

See *Sugar Syrup, Fruit*

PEAS

MANGE TOUT

Mange tout peas are cooked to perfection in the microwave, retaining their colour and crispness well. Wash and drain 450 g (1 lb) mange tout and place in a bowl with 25 g (1 oz) butter. Cover and microwave on 100% High for 4–5 minutes, tossing twice during cooking. Season and stand for 2 minutes.

Serve with white sauce or toss with crisply fried bacon pieces.

PEPPERS

Prepare stuffed peppers and place in a deep casserole dish. Cover and microwave on 100% High for 5 minutes. Rearrange, turn dish and microwave for a further 5 minutes. Serve with tomato sauce.

The skins of microwaved peppers may be slightly tougher than when conventionally cooked, but time and flavour loss is reduced as they do not need to be blanched before cooking.

See *Sauces, Tomato*

PIES

See *Pastry*

PIZZAS

If fresh or frozen pizzas are microwaved on a prepared browning dish they will retain a crisp bottom and brown underneath. Do not slice a pizza on a browning dish as it could damage the surface.

Browning dishes are not essential when cooking pizzas. They can be cooked on any suitable dish or plate. If cooked on a roasting rack the dough will be drier as the steam can escape underneath. To give a fresh pizza dough base a crunchier crust, brush the plate with melted butter and sprinkle it with breadcrumbs, poppy seeds, or sesame seeds before placing the dough on it.

Microwave a 20 cm (8 inch) pizza on 100% High for 4–6 minutes. If cooking on a browning dish increase the cooking time by 1–2 minutes, checking to see that the bottom does not overcook. If possible top the pizza with grated cheese 2 minutes before the end of the cooking time so that it does not toughen and overcook.

DEEP DISH PIZZA

When making deep dish pizzas, press the prepared dough into a deep plate 20–24 cm (8–10 inch) in diameter and leave to rise for 30 minutes. Microwave on 100% High for 3–4 minutes until the base is dry but still spongy. Fill the pizza with cooked meat filling, sprinkle with cheese and microwave on 100% High for 2–3 minutes more. Sprinkle with chopped parsley after cooking.

QUICK PIZZA

Rub 175 g (6 oz) plain flour, 50 g (2 oz) margarine and 2 tsp mixed herbs together. Bind with 4 tbsp milk. Roll out to a 20 cm (8 inch) diameter and lay on a plate or a flat dish.

Mix together 75 g (3 oz) grated cheese, 50 g (2 oz) chopped ham or continental sausage and 2 tbsp tomato ketchup. Spread on the pizza base and microwave on 100% High for 2½–3½ minutes. Substitute half brown for white flour if wished. This pizza will have a crisper base if cooked on a browning dish and is best served cold with salad.

Use split muffins, French sticks, crumpets, rolls, melba toast, scones etc. to make snack pizzas in seconds. Just top them with a jar of ready prepared pizza topping, sprinkle with cheese and microwave on 100% High until hot and the cheese melted.

See *Scones, Dough*

PLUMS

See *Fruit, Poaching*

POPCORN

It is safest to use a specially designed corn popper to avoid any damage to the magnetron in the cooker.

CHOC FRUIT AND NUT

Add chopped nuts and cherries to cooked popcorn. Bind together with some melted chocolate. Spoon into paper cake cases and leave to set.

REHEATING

Place approximately 1 litre (2 pt) popped corn in a large bowl and microwave uncovered on 100% High for 1 minute until warm, tossing once.

For toffee-coated popcorn, heat 125 g (4 oz) sugar with 150 ml (¼ pt) water in a large bowl or jug and microwave on 100% High for 2 minutes, stirring twice during cooking. Make sure the sugar has completely dissolved and microwave the syrup on 100% High for a further 8–10 minutes until golden brown. Take care because the syrup is extremely hot. Pour over the popcorn and toss well to give a crispy coating.

SAVOURY

Season cooked popcorn while still warm with a sprinkling of salt, curry powder or paprika and serve with party drinks.

POPPADUMS

Place two or three poppadums on the cooker base and microwave on 100% High for 45–60 seconds until puffy. Cool on a rack for a few seconds before serving.

Poppadums may also be lightly brushed with oil on both sides. Microwave one for 20–25 seconds on 100% High, turning over once during cooking. Place on kitchen paper to cool before serving.

PORRIDGE

Porridge can be made easily in the serving dish with no sticky pan to wash. Place 120 g (8 tbsp) easy cook rolled oats in a bowl. Add a pinch of salt, 300 ml (½ pt) water or milk and water mixed and stir well. Microwave on 100% High for 3 minutes, stirring twice during cooking. Stand covered for 1 minute, stir well and serve with sugar, honey or syrup.

SCOTTISH

To make a traditional Scottish porridge, use medium or coarse oatmeal instead of rolled oats.

Place 90 g (6 tbsp) oatmeal in a bowl. Add a pinch of salt, 450 ml (¾ pt) water or milk and water mixed and stir well. Microwave on 100% High for 4–6 minutes, stirring twice during cooking. Stand covered for 1 minute, stir well and serve with soft brown sugar and a topping of cream.

POTATOES

CHIPS

Oven chips may be cooked on a browning dish in the microwave with excellent results. Prepare the dish to the manufacturer's instructions and coat lightly with oil. Cook two portions of chips on 100% High for 3–5 minutes, tossing two or three times during cooking.

DICED

Cook diced potatoes for use in salads. Place 225 g (8 oz) diced potatoes (skins left on) in a dish with 1 tbsp water. Cover and microwave for 2–3 minutes. Toss and microwave for a further 2–3 minutes. Leave to stand for 2 minutes. Cool and add to salad recipes or serve with a salad dressing or mayonnaise.

JACKET

Wash and pierce the skin of a 125–175 g (4–6 oz) potato. Place on a piece of kitchen paper inside the cooker and microwave on 100% High for 4–6 minutes, turning over halfway through cooking time.

Jacket potatoes will stay piping hot for half an hour if wrapped in foil after cooking. (Do *not* reheat in foil.)

Reheat jacket potatoes by wrapping securely in clingfilm. Microwave on 100% High for 30–45 seconds for each potato and they will taste freshly cooked.

NEW

A few drops of lemon juice added to the water before cooking new potatoes will prevent them from turning black around the edges. Pierce the skins or score round the centre before cooking to prevent the skins from bursting.

POULTRY

Brush uncooked poultry with melted butter or margarine and sprinkle with colour enhancers (see *Browning Agents*). Place in a pierced roasting bag on a dish and microwave on 100% High for 6 minutes per 450 g (1 lb). Cook whole large birds upside down on each side before turning breast uppermost to ensure even cooking.

See *Chicken*

PRAWNS

See *Shellfish*

PRESERVES

See *Citrus, Curds, Jam, Marmalade*

PRUNES

It is not necessary to pre-soak prunes when cooked in the microwave. Place 225 g (8 oz) prunes in a dish with enough water or cold tea to cover them. Cover and microwave on 100% High for 4–5 minutes, stirring once during cooking. Stand for 5 minutes to plump up before serving.

PUDDINGS

When microwaving suet and sponge puddings, remove clingfilm covering as soon as they are cooked so that it does not contract and squash them. Microwaved puddings are much lighter in texture and rise more than when conventionally cooked, but they tend to dry out much quicker. They can be refreshed once by reheating if eaten immediately.

When reheating steamed puddings, moisture may easily be lost. For best results, arrange a single layer of slices round the edge of a plate, placing a glass of water in the centre. Cover loosely with clingfilm. Microwave on 100% High for 1–2½ minutes or until the underside of the plate feels warm to touch. Slices may also be wrapped individually in clingfilm and warmed as above without the water.

MILK

As a general rule, use 50 g (2 oz) grain, e.g. rice, semolina, tapioca, to 600 ml (1 pt) liquid and 2 tbsp sugar. Cook on 50% Medium power to reduce the risk of boiling over.

RICE

Rice puddings can be made in the microwave, but will not have a brown skin on the surface. They are creamier than when conventionally cooked and the texture slightly thicker. To assist in softening the grains of rice for a creamier pudding, soak them in the cooking liquid overnight.

Place 50 g (2 oz) short grain rice in a large bowl with 600 ml (1 pt) milk and 2 tbsp sugar. Cover and microwave on 100% High for 4–5 minutes until boiling, stirring once. Reduce to 50% Medium and microwave for a further 30–35 minutes, stirring twice during cooking. Stand for 5 minutes. Stir well and serve.

Substitute 150 ml (¼ pt) of the milk with evaporated or condensed milk for a richer pudding. If using condensed milk, omit the sugar.

Add cinnamon, mixed spice, lemon or orange zest, vanilla sugar for a flavoured pudding.

Add chopped, dried fruit, sultanas or nuts to the pudding halfway through cooking time for a more interesting pudding.

Most grain puddings can be made using this method.

SPONGE

Do not microwave sponge pudding recipes that use a covering of syrup, honey, jam, or high sugar content ingredient in the bottom of the basin. Microwave energy is attracted to sugars causing them to burn with prolonged heating.

When making a pudding using a fresh fruit base, microwave on medium power to stop moisture being drawn from the fruit and making the sponge wet and soggy.

A layer of breadcrumbs sprinkled over fruit or liquid in the bottom of the pudding will absorb moisture and prevent it being soggy. Add up to 1 tbsp more liquid to sponge pudding recipes when cooking in the microwave. Only half fill the basin with mixture and cover loosely with vented clingfilm. A 125 g (4 oz) sponge mixture will take 4–6 minutes on 100% High to cook.

Microwaved puddings sometimes look undercooked and soft on the top. To check if they are done, leave to stand for 5 minutes and test with a skewer. Return to the cooker for a few seconds more if they are undercooked. Prepare dishes and basins as for cakes.

SUET

Suet puddings cook extremely well in the microwave. They are lighter in texture than when conventionally cooked, but the greatest advantage is that they cook in minutes without filling the kitchen with condensation.

Improve the appearance of a sweet pudding by sprinkling toasted breadcrumbs or biscuit crumbs inside the basin before cooking. Loosely cover the surface of a pudding before cooking with vented clingfilm to assist in retaining the moisture. Never fill to the top of the basin and leave at least 2.5 cm (1 inch) to allow for the pudding to rise. Stand for 5 minutes before serving. A suet pudding should be well risen and puffy, and the top appear flaky when cooked.

Layers of fruit and suet pastry placed in a pudding basin produce very good results when cooked. A 225 g (8 oz) recipe will take 6–8 minutes on 100% High to cook.

To microwave a jam roll using 225 g (8 oz) suet pastry, place the roll seam down on a sheet of lightly greased greaseproof paper and microwave on 100% high for 4–5 minutes. Brown under a grill and sprinkle with sugar to serve.

See *Dumplings, Sauces*

YORKSHIRE PUDDING

Yorkshire puddings cannot be made in a microwave but they can be reheated. Place four cooked Yorkshires in a circle on a sheet of kitchen paper. Microwave on 100% High for 20–30 seconds.

PULSES

It is better to cook pulses by the conventional method as there is hardly any timesaving and often the outer covering of the pulses burst during microwaving.

See *Kidney Beans*

Q

QUICHE

Quiche can be cooked successfully in the microwave, if a 50% Medium power setting is used.

Microwave a 20 cm (8 inch) pastry case and fill with ingredients of your choice. Beat the eggs, milk and seasonings together and pour over the filling. Microwave for 15–20 minutes on 50% Medium, turning the dish four times during cooking. Stand for 5 minutes and brown the top under a hot grill to improve the appearance.

See *Pastry*

R

RATATOUILLE

Ratatouille is easily made in the microwave as the vegetables can cook in their own juices if preferred. Microwave the onions and butter for 1½–2 minutes before adding the other ingredients and cook in a covered dish for 8–10 minutes, stirring twice during cooking. Season and leave to stand for 3–4 minutes before serving.

Garnish with parsley and serve hot as a vegetable or leave to cool, chill in the refrigerator and serve as a salad.

There is no time saved when cooking rice in the microwave, but it results in fluffy, separate grains.

For salads, cool the rice and add salad dressings. Garnish with lemon wedges and parsley. Serve chilled.

Brown or white rice may be flavoured with tomato purée, curry paste, herbs or add cooked vegetables, sultanas, cheese, etc. for a more interesting variation.

To cook 175 g (6 oz) long grain rice, place in a large casserole with 400 ml (14 fl oz) boiling salted water. Cover with a loose lid and microwave on 100% High for 12–14 minutes, stirring once during cooking. Stand for 3 minutes. All the liquid will be absorbed and the rice just needs fluffing up with a fork before serving.

BROWN RICE

To cook 175 g (6 oz) brown rice use the method above but microwave for 20–25 minutes. Stand for 3 minutes, fluff up and use as required.

If your microwave has a variable control, cook the rice for 2–3 minutes on 100% High, then reduce to 50% Medium. Add 5–10 minutes to the timings if using this method. Microwaving the rice on a medium setting will reduce the risk of the water boiling over.

REHEATING

Rice can be reheated successfully too: place two portions of cooked rice in a covered dish and microwave on 100% High for 2–3 minutes. Toss well to separate the grains and serve.

See *Puddings*

ROASTING BAGS

See *Covering Food*

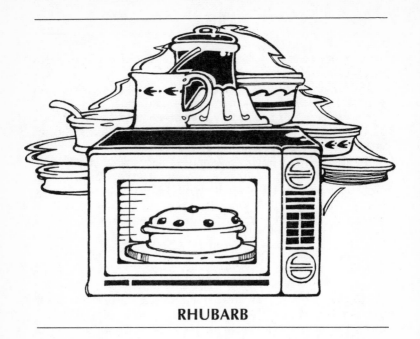

RHUBARB

BLANCHING

Prepare 450 g (1 lb) as for cooking (below) and microwave on 100% High for 2–3 minutes, tossing halfway through cooking time.

COOKING

There is no mushy result when cooked in the microwave. Cut 350 g (12 oz) washed rhubarb into 2.5 cm (1 inch) pieces and place in a dish with 2 tbsp water. Cover loosely and microwave on 100% High for 5–6 minutes, tossing halfway through cooking time. Stir in 125 g (4 oz) sugar and 1 tsp lemon juice. Stand covered for 3 minutes before serving.

ROLLS

See *Bread*

S

SAFETY

Never switch on a microwave when it is empty as it could damage the components.

Keep a cup of water inside the cooker to prevent this happening.

SALT

DRYING

To dry damp salt, place in a bowl and microwave on 100% High for 20–40 seconds.

SEASONING

Season food with salt after it has been microwaved as it can toughen and dry out some foods if added before.

SAUCES

Sauces can be made in advance and reheated (covered) when required. This is a great advantage if entertaining as they can be warmed in the serving dish. For a speedy sauce, heat a tin of condensed soup.

BASIC WHITE

Melt 25 g (1 oz) butter, stir in 25 g (1 oz) plain flour and blend in 300 ml (½ pt) milk. Microwave on 100% High for 3–4 minutes, whisking twice during cooking. Season with salt and pepper. Serve with vegetables or fish.

The sauce can be enriched when cooked by adding 15–25 g (½–1 oz) butter or 4 tbsp cream, or beating in 1 egg yolk (make sure the sauce is not boiling). Alternatively, add one of the following:

Cheese Add 75–125 g (3–4 oz) to the basic sauce. Heat for a few seconds if necessary to melt the cheese.

Egg Add 2 chopped, hard-boiled eggs.

Mushroom Add 50 g (2 oz) sliced cooked mushrooms.

Onion Add 1 chopped and cooked onion.

Parsley Add 2 tbsp chopped parsley.

Prawn Add 50 g (2 oz) prawns and 1 tsp lemon juice.

BREAD

Mix half a grated onion, 50 g (2 oz) fresh breadcrumbs, 25 g (1 oz) butter, 150 ml (¼ pt) milk, 1 bay leaf, pinch of nutmeg, salt and pepper, in a bowl. Microwave on 50% Medium for 3–4 minutes, stirring halfway through cooking time. Remove bay leaf, stir well and serve. The sauce may be flavoured with clove instead of nutmeg.

CRANBERRY

Place 250 g (8 oz) cranberries, 150 ml (¼ pt) water, 175 g (6 oz) granulated sugar, 1 tsp lemon juice and the grated rind of half a lemon in a bowl. Mix well, cover and microwave on 100% High for 6–8 minutes. Stir and crush the cranberries two or three times during cooking. Then microwave on Low (Defrost) for a further 6–8 minutes, stirring and crushing as before. Cover and leave to cool to thicken the sauce. Serve with chicken, turkey or gammon.

TOMATO

Place 25 g (1 oz) butter, 1 chopped small red or green pepper and 1 small onion in a bowl. Cover and microwave on 100% High for 2 minutes, stirring once during cooking. Add 1 x 439 g (15 oz) tin of chopped tomatoes, 3 tbsp tomato purée, 2 tsp brown sugar, ½ tsp thyme and ½ tsp oregano. Mix well and microwave uncovered on 100% High for 3–4 minutes.

If a thinner sauce is required add a little stock. Liquidize the sauce if preferred.

Serve with stuffed peppers, aubergines, courgettes, onions and marrow.

SWEET SAUCES

ARROWROOT

An arrowroot sauce can be made quickly in the microwave and used to put a glaze on fruit flans or serve with ice-creams and sponge puddings. Blend 4 tsp arrowroot with 2 tbsp water. Microwave 300 ml (½ pt) canned fruit juice or pure fruit juice (top up with water if necessary) on 100% High for 2–3 minutes until just starting to boil. Pour on to arrowroot mixture and stir well. Microwave on 100% High for ½–1 minute until thick, stirring twice during cooking. Add sugar to sweeten if needed. The sauce may be flavoured with orange or lemon juice and add a few drops of colouring to improve its colour. Cool before glazing flans.

CARAMEL

Place 225 g (8 oz) caramel sweets and 6 tbsp milk in a bowl.

Microwave on 50% Medium for 2–3 minutes until the caramel has melted. Stir four times during cooking. Serve with sponge puddings or ice-cream.

CHERRY AND ALMOND

Place 50 g (2 oz) unsalted butter and 4 tbsp golden syrup in a bowl. Cover and microwave on 100% High for 1–1½ minutes until melted and hot. Add 50 g (2 oz) flaked almonds and 50 g (2 oz) chopped glacé cherries. Stir well and serve with sponge and suet puddings.

CLEAR LEMON OR ORANGE

Place 2 tsp cornflour, 125 g (4 oz) sugar, 50 g (2 oz) unsalted butter and the grated rind and juice of 1 orange or lemon in a bowl. Mix in 300 ml (½ pt) water and microwave on 100% High for 2–2½ minutes, whisking twice during cooking. Cook for a further 1½–2 minutes and whisk again.

FRUIT

To make delicious sauces for puddings and ice-creams, use canned fruit syrup made up to 300 ml (½ pt) with water. Blend in 1 tbsp cornflour and microwave on 100% High for 3–4 minutes, whisking halfway during cooking. And a few drops of colouring to improve the appearance if pale juices are used.

JAM

Heat jam in a jug on 100% High for a few seconds to make measuring and pouring sauces easier.

For a thinner jam sauce use equal quantities of jam and water with a few drops of lemon. Microwave on 100% High for 1 minute, stirring once during cooking.

MARSHMALLOW

Place 125 g (4 oz) marshmallows and 2 tbsp evaporated milk in a bowl and microwave on 50% Medium for 1½–2 minutes. Stir well and serve hot with ice-cream. Flavour the sauce with coffee, chocolate or essence.

QUICK CHOCOLATE

Place 125 g (4 oz) white, milk or plain chocolate in a bowl with 15 g (½ oz) butter, 2 tbsp water, 2 tbsp golden syrup. Microwave on 100% High for 2–3 minutes. This sauce will thicken on cooling. Serve hot with ice-cream or choux pastries. For variations use a flavoured chocolate, e.g. orange, or replace the water with brandy or rum.

SWEET WHITE

Place 15 g (½ oz) cornflour, 15 g (½ oz) butter and 1 tbsp caster sugar in a bowl. Blend in 300 ml (½ pt) milk and microwave on 100% High for 2–2½ minutes, whisking twice during cooking. Cook for a further 1½–2 minutes. Whisk again and flavour with vanilla, almond, brandy or rum essences, melted chocolate or coffee. Serve with sponge and suet puddings.

See *Cakes, Fillings and Toppings*

SAUSAGES

Sausages can be cooked in the microwave but will not colour without using a browning dish.

Prick the skins to break the membrane and prevent them from bursting. Brush 450 g (1 lb) sausages with a browning agent and place on a shallow dish lined with kitchen paper. Place another sheet on the top to absorb any spitting and microwave on 100% High for 5–6 minutes, rearranging once during cooking.

To make sausages look more appetizing, wrap a rasher of streaky bacon round each sausage before cooking and microwave.

CONTINENTAL

Boiling sausage rings can be microwaved in their plastic packaging. Pierce the bag and skin of an 225 g (8 oz) sausage. Place in a dish and microwave on 100% High for 1–1½ minutes. Turn the sausage over and cook for a further 1½ minutes. Stand for 2 minutes before serving.

SCONES

Scones can be cooked successfully in the microwave but tend to dry out more quickly than when conventionally cooked, so are best eaten when they are fresh and warm. As scones will not brown in the microwave, brush the tops with melted butter before cooking and sprinkle with breadcrumbs, biscuit crumbs, oats, spice, or brown under a hot grill after cooking. Add dried fruit and spices to the ingredients or a mixture of brown and white flour.

COOKING

To microwave eight scones, place in a circle on a sheet of greaseproof paper or shallow dish. Microwave on 100% High for 4–5 minutes until risen and springy when touched. Serve warm, split and buttered with jam or syrup.

Scones can be cooked on a browning dish and will look more appealing. Omit sprinkling the tops with breadcrumbs but still brush with butter before cooking. Prepare the browning dish, brush with oil and place the scones on it. Microwave on 100% High for 1½–2 minutes. Turn the scones over and microwave for a further 1½–2 minutes. Cool and dust with icing sugar.

SAVOURY

Add grated cheese, herbs, savoury spice, mustard, chopped bacon etc. to a basic savoury scone mixture and cook as before. Sprinkle the tops of the scones with the same ingredients before microwaving to improve their appearance. If using cheese as a topping, sprinkle over the scones halfway through cooking.

Scone dough can also be used as a pizza base and cooked successfully in the microwave. Microwave a 20 cm (8 inch) base on 100% High for 2 minutes. Arrange slices of ham, tomato, olives, etc. on the top and sprinkle with herbs and grated cheese. Microwave on 100% High until the cheese starts to melt.

SEASONINGS

Microwaving food intensifies all flavours, so use seasonings, herbs and spices very carefully, reducing the quantity when using conventional recipes for microwave cookery.

SESAME SEEDS

Toast sesame seeds by placing a few tablespoons in a shallow dish. Microwave on 100% High, tossing several times during cooking until golden brown. Use to decorate breads, vegetables, pastry dishes, etc.

SHELLFISH

Microwave energy is able to pass through the outer casing of shellfish as they do a covered dish. Because of this the full flavour of shellfish is appreciated.

MUSSELS

Cook and eat mussels on the day of purchase. Discard any

before cooking if their shells are open and will not close when tapped.

Scrub the mussels, remove any barnacles with a knife and pull away the beards. Place 450 g (1 lb) mussels, 15 g (½ oz) butter, 150 ml (¼ pt) dry white wine, 1 small onion, finely chopped, 1 garlic clove, crushed, and 1 tbsp chopped parsley in a bowl.

Cover and microwave on 100% High for approximately 3 minutes until the shells begin to open. Stir halfway through cooking time. Serve immediately with the juices and a sprinkling of fresh parsley. Mop up the liquor with warm crusty bread.

PRAWNS

Place 450 g (1 lb) fresh unpeeled prawns in a dish with 600 ml (1 pt) water, 2 bay leaves, salt and pepper. Cover and microwave on 100% High for 6–8 minutes until boiling. Stir halfway through cooking time. Stand for 1–2 minutes, then drain and cool. To reduce the fishy smell during cooking, add 1 tbsp vinegar to the water.

SHRIMPS

Use the method above, but microwave for 5–7 minutes.

SHORTBREAD

Shortbread can be made in the microwave but will not give as good a result than when conventionally cooked. Cream 100 g (4 oz) butter with 50 g (2 oz) caster sugar. Add 175 g (6 oz) plain flour and mix to form a soft dough. Press into a lightly greased 18–20 cm (7–8 inch) shallow dish. Prick the base well and pinch the edges with finger and thumb. Microwave on 100% High for 4–5 minutes. Leave to cool slightly, mark into triangles and sprinkle with sugar. Serve with mousses and fools or eat as a biscuit.

SHRIMPS

See *Shellfish*

SKIN

Prick, score or cut all foods that are enclosed in a skin or membrane before microwaving, e.g. tomatoes, potatoes, apples, liver, kidneys, fish, eggs, etc. Failure to do this will cause them to burst.

SOUP

When making conventional soup recipes in the microwave, remember to reduce the cooking liquid by up to half as there is less evaporation. Do not overseason as seasonings are intensified. Add hot stock or liquid to reduce the cooking time. Place the ingredients in a deep casserole to avoid boiling over, cover and cook on 100% High. Stir occasionally during cooking. Serve soup with flavoured French bread, croûtons or dumplings.

Pour a can of soup into a mug or bowl, cover and microwave on 100% High for 2–3 minutes. Stir once during cooking.

See *Bread, French, Croûtons* and *Dumplings*

SPAGHETTI

See *Pasta*

SPEEDY SNACKS

HAMBURGERS

Microwave one 125 g (4 oz) hamburger on 100% High for 1 minute each side. Stand for 1 minute and serve in a warmed bun with relish or mustard.

HOT DOG ROLLS

Prick four hot dog sausages and place in soft rolls. Wrap in kitchen paper and microwave on 100% High for 1½–2½ minutes. Serve with relish, ketchup, mustard, or fried onions.

HOT FILLED ROLLS

Fill four crusty rolls with filling of choice, wrap in kitchen paper and microwave as before. Serve with coleslaw and salad.
See *Bread, Toasted sandwiches and Pitta bread*, and *Croissants*

SPICES

To avoid spices having a raw taste especially when using them in foreign recipes, microwave with a little oil on 100% High for a few seconds before adding them to the other ingredients.

See *Seasonings*

SPINACH

The microwave cooks spinach well. As no added water is used most of the nutrients and vitamins are retained.

Wash 450 g (1 lb) spinach and drain well. Place whole or chopped leaves in a pierced boiling or roasting bag with a knob of butter. Microwave on 100% High for 6–8 minutes, tossing once during cooking. Season, toss again and leave to stand for 2 minutes. Spinach may also be cooked in a covered dish using the same method.

SPRING GREENS

Wash, drain and cut away stalks. Shred the leaves and microwave as for spinach above.

STANDING TIME

Standing time is an important factor of microwave cookery, because food continues to cook during that period. Generally allow one third of the cooking time when leaving food to stand, but denser food will take longer. If cooking more than one food, e.g. jacket potatoes, the standing time need not be increased as this is catered for in the cooking time.

See *Foil*

STERILIZING

Sterilize jars to use for preserving by putting 150 ml (¼ pt) water into each jar. Microwave on 100% High until boiling and continue to heat for 1 minute. Remove the jars using oven gloves, pour out water and place open end down on kitchen paper. The hot jars can then be filled with preserves. Do not use this method for sterilizing babies' bottles and teats.

STIR-FRY

Stir-fry recipes work very well in the microwave. The cooking time is roughly the same as the conventional method, but smells are cut to a minimum, less stirring is required and the vegetables retain their colour, crispness and flavour.

Meat can be added to the vegetables, but ensure that all ingredients are cut to a uniform size to assist in even cooking. Cook the stir-fry in a browning dish for a slightly better result.

Microwave a vegetable stir-fry recipe uncovered for 4 servings on 100% High for 4–6 minutes, stirring twice during cooking. Microwave strips of meat on 100% High for 2–3 minutes, then continue as above when cooking meat stir-frys.

STOCKS

Use hot water when making stocks in the microwave. Place the ingredients in a deep casserole to avoid boiling over and cover with a lid to prevent evaporation.

Fish stock – microwave on 100% High for 8–10 minutes.
Meat bone – microwave on 100% High for 30–40 minutes.
Poultry – microwave on 100% High for 15–20 minutes.

STUFFINGS

BACON

Place 25 g (1 oz) butter in a bowl with 50 g (2 oz) chopped bacon, 1 chopped onion, 1 finely chopped carrot and microwave covered on 100% High for 2 minutes, stirring once halfway through cooking time. Add salt and pepper, 1 tsp chopped parsley and 50 g (2 oz) fresh breadcrumbs. Mix well and use to stuff chicken, lamb and pork joints.

RICE

Mix together 125 g (4 oz) cooked long grain rice, 1 chopped cooked onion, 50 g (2 oz) chopped cooked mushrooms, salt and pepper, 1 tsp dried herbs. Use to stuff vegetables, e.g. marrow, aubergines, peppers, onions.

SUGAR

DRYING

To dry damp sugar, place 125 g (4 oz) in a bowl and microwave on 100% High for 20–40 seconds.

SOFTENING

To soften brown sugar which has gone hard, place 225 g (8 oz) in a boiling bag and sprinkle with water or add a slice of apple. Tie loosely and microwave on 100% High for 30 seconds. Check halfway through cooking time. Leave to stand for 5 minutes before use.

SYRUP

Sugar syrups are basically used for poaching fresh fruits.

To make a light syrup, place 125 g (4 oz) sugar and 300 ml (½ pt) water in a bowl and microwave on 100% High for approximately 4 minutes until boiling. Stir every minute during cooking to ensure that the sugar dissolves.

Light syrup is suitable for poaching the 'sweeter' fruits, e.g. peaches, plums, nectarines, apricots, greengages, etc.

A heavier syrup may be required for poaching the 'tart' fruits, e.g. rhubarb, cooking apples, gooseberries. Use the same method as above, but increase the sugar to 175 g (6 oz).

A sugar syrup may be flavoured and coloured to improve the appearance and taste of the fruit when it is poached:

Red wine   Substitute red wine for water when making a light syrup. A dash of lemon juice will improve the flavour. This syrup is particularly good for poaching pears as they turn a rich red colour.

Spiced   Add a cinnamon stick and a few cloves. Strain the juice before using to poach apples.

SYRUP SAUCE, LIQUEUR

Make a light syrup sauce, reducing the water by 2 tbsp. Add 2 tbsp liqueur to the hot sauce and serve or use as required. The sauce may be coloured to improve its appearance.

Amaretto   Serve with peaches, nectarines, apricots, greengages. Decorate with ratafia biscuits or flaked biscuits.

Orange liqueur or Curaçao   Serve with pineapple, oranges, apricots, peaches.

Cherry brandy   Serve with red or black cherries, raspberries, pineapple, plums.

Apricot brandy   Serve with oranges, apricots, peaches.

Kirsch   Serve with red or black cherries, pineapple, greengages.

SYRUP SAUCE, SPIRIT

Spirits may also be used to flavour a light syrup sauce.

Brandy   Serve with oranges, apricots, peaches, bananas.

Dark or white rum   Serve with oranges, pears, bananas.

Vodka   Serve with raspberries, pears, pineapple, greengages.

SWEETCORN

Place two corn on the cob in a dish with 4 tbsp water and a knob of butter. Cover and microwave on 100% High for 6–8 minutes, turning over halfway through cooking time. Leave to stand for 1 minute. To reheat whole sweetcorn, wrap securely in clingfilm and microwave one cob for 45–60 seconds to taste as good as freshly cooked.

SWEDES

See *Parsnips*

SYRUP

CRYSTALLIZED

To heat crystallized syrup, remove the metal lid from the jar and microwave on 50% Medium or Low (Defrost) for a few seconds to regain a smooth liquid.

MEASURING

Heat syrup in a jug for a few seconds on 100% High to make measuring easier.

See *Sugar*

T

TEA

A cup or mug of tea may be reheated in the microwave from cold and the flavour will not be affected. Heat on 100% High for 1½–2 minutes.

TEABREADS

See *Bread, Defrosting*

TEMPERATURE PROBE

A temperature probe is a specially designed thermometer for use in a microwave cooker. It determines the internal temperature of food, which is particularly useful when cooking joints of meat to test if they are cooked. Follow the manufacturer's instructions for their use.

Never use conventional meat or sugar thermometers in a microwave.

TOAST

To reheat cold buttered toast, place one slice on a sheet of kitchen paper and microwave on 100% High for 15 seconds.

TOMATOES

COOKING

To microwave four whole tomatoes, cut a small cross on the

base of the fruit and place in a dish stalk end down. Cover loosely with clingfilm and microwave on 100% High for 2–2½ minutes. Stand for 1 minute before serving.

PEELING

To peel easily, prick the skins of 1 kg (2 lb) tomatoes, place in a bowl and cover with boiling water. Microwave on 100% High for 30 seconds or until the skins begin to shrink from the flesh. Drain, cover with cold water and leave for 1 minute before skinning.

TURKEY

Follow the same basic rules as preparing and cooking chicken, but only stuff the neck and never the body cavity. Make sure there is at least a 5 cm (2 inch) gap between the turkey and the walls of the cooker. Microwave on 100% High for 9–11 minutes per 450 g (1 lb) or 11–13 minutes on 50% Medium. Stand in foil, shiny side inwards, for 30 minutes before carving. Serve with bread or cranberry sauce.

See *Chicken, Sauces*

TURNIPS

See *Parsnips*

U

UTENSILS

Do not leave metal spoons, forks, whisks, foil, etc. in the cooker when the microwave is in use.

Wooden spoons can be left in the microwave when making sauces or custards for short periods of time.

See *Dishes*

V

VEGETABLES

BLANCHING

Prepare 450 g (1 lb) washed and drained vegetables and place in a dish with 3 tbsp water. Cover and microwave on 100% High for 3 minutes, tossing halfway through cooking time. Place in a bowl of iced water until cold. Drain well and open freeze.

COOKING

Small quantities of frozen vegetables can be cooked in a freezer bag. Pierce the bag of a 225 g (8 oz) packet, place on a sheet of kitchen paper and microwave as usual.

Frozen vegetables may also be cooked in a serving dish, so reducing washing up.

MATCHSTICK

For a variation in cooking vegetables, cut them into match-stick-sized pieces 7.5 cm (3 inch) long.

To cook four servings, place 25 g (1 oz) butter in a dish and microwave on 100% High for 30 seconds, until melted. Add 225 g (8 oz) matchstick vegetables, cover and microwave on 100% High for 5–6 minutes, tossing once during cooking.

Season and leave to stand for 2 minutes before serving. Garnish with chopped parsley.

For speed, use a potato peeler to slice the vegetables instead of cutting into matchsticks.

REHEATING

Vegetables will reheat more quickly if covered with pierced clingfilm or a lid to retain their moisture.

See *individual vegetables, Stir-fry*

VINEGAR

FLAVOURED

Place a sprig of fresh herbs of your choice in a bottle or jar e.g. mint, tarragon, thyme or a mixture. Cover with 300–600 ml (½–1 pt) distilled malt vinegar and microwave on 100% High for ½–1½ minutes until just warm. Check regularly. Seal with a plastic lid and store in a cool, dark place for two weeks before using.

After opening, store in a refrigerator for up to eight weeks. Garlic and onion can also be used as flavourings, and cider vinegar instead of malt. Use when making marinades, salad dressings or mayonnaise.

W

WATER

See *Liquids*

WINE

Bring cold wine to room temperature by pouring into a large jug or heatproof carafe and microwave on 100% High for a few seconds.

MULLED

Pour 1 litre (1¾ pt) wine into a bowl. Add 125 g (4 oz) soft brown sugar, 6 cloves, 3 cinnamon sticks, pinch of mixed spice, 1 sliced orange and 1 sliced lemon. Mix well and microwave on 100% High for 5–7 minutes, stirring halfway through cooking to ensure the sugar is completely dissolved. Add a spirit of your choice after microwaving and strain if preferred.

WINE AND LIQUEURS IN DRINKS

When heating a drink containing alcohol, cover with pierced clingfilm to prevent excess evaporation and do not allow it to reach boiling point.

See *Flambéeing*

Y

YORKSHIRE PUDDINGS

See *Puddings*

Z

ZEST

See *Citrus, Zest*

NOTES

NOTES

NOTES

been established, he used the pattern—though he usually transcended it. Before studying *Lycidas,* one should read at least three pastoral elegies written by the Sicilians, to see what patterns they had established: Idyl I of Theocritus, with the lament of the shepherd Thyrsis for his lost companion, Daphnis; Idyl I of Bion, "The Lament for Adonis," the youth beloved by Venus, who had been gored to death by a boar; Idyl III of Moschus, "The Lament for Bion" who had apparently met his death through poison. We notice at once one device used by all three which is not in *Lycidas* but which Milton used in his Latin pastoral elegy on the death of Charles Diodati, *Epitaphium Damonis,:* the refrain, which marks the stanzaic form, usually beginning with a line like, "Begin ye Muses dear, begin the shepherd's song," and changing toward the end to, "Give o'er, ye Muses dear, now cease the shepherd's song." Each of the classical poets begins by indicating the reason for his song—the death of a shepherd. Each suggests what might be called "the lament of Nature" for the dead shepherd. Sometimes the mourning is of animals—wolves, jackals, lions; often it is the lament of trees or flowers, nightingales and swans, or such aspects of Nature as rivers, caves, mountains. Frequently we hear the names of flowers, sometimes in a passage in which they are brought to deck the bier of the dead. Like Nature, the gods come to mourn and praise the shepherd. "Came Hermes first from the hill. . . . Came also Priapus. . . . Yea, and Galatea laments thy song. . . . And the Satyrs mourned thee, and the Priape in sable raiment, and the Panes sorrow for thy song." The lament of Nature, the flower passages, the procession of mourners—these had all been further developed by poets who had followed the tradition which Milton had inherited. We shall find them in *Lycidas* interwoven with other patterns and designs to make a whole which, while purposely derivative, is unique in poetry. Enough for introduction: let us turn to the poem.

Analysis of *Lycidas*

"In this monody the author bewails a learned friend"—we are familiar with the circumstances so that I need not labor the little prose-introduction except to call your attention to the word "monody," to which we shall return. Like the classical writers before him, Milton begins by stating the reason for writing. A shepherd has died, a shepherd who had sung his songs, a young shepherd who had not come to maturity. The shepherd who remains must gather leaves to make the wreaths classical writers associated with funerals, leaves of evergreen plants, laurel, myrtle, ivy. Laurel, we know, was a symbol of triumph, the laurel wreath given to the victor, whether he lived or died. Myrtle, with its darker leaf, is a symbol of mourning. Listen for those two motifs as we go on —triumph and lament. But, because the death was untimely, the plants themselves had not yet ripened. The berries are still harsh and crude, and the fingers of the shepherd are forced to tear them rudely "before the mellowing year." Lycidas is dead, dead ere his prime. What shepherd-poet would refuse to sing a song in memory of the shepherd who was himself a poet? The lines that follow (12-14) echo the belief of our classical ancestors that the spirits of the dead would not rest in peace unless some reverence was paid to the body, a belief deeply embedded in primitive and sophisticated alike, lying behind customs like funerals or memorial services. If you have read the *Antigone* of Sophocles, you will remember that this custom of paying reverence to a dead body lay behind the tragedy of Antigone, torn between the law of the state which had forbidden any kind of burial rites to Polynices and the filial piety of a sister who must do something—even scatter earth or ashes upon the corpse—so that her brother's soul might rest. No reverence could be paid to the body of Edward King who had been drowned at sea but symbolically his brother-shepherds could bring their wreaths of laurel and myrtle (their memorial volume) as their sad service.

Like his classical models, Milton uses an invocation to the Muses: "Begin then, Sisters of the sacred well." The Muses, like many gods, might be invoked at various places. Why did Milton specifically localize them at the Pierian spring? The answer is important, and leads to a reiterated device in *Lycidas*. As you will see, this is a *water-poem,* filled with water-images, peculiarly suitable for a poem on the death of a young man drowned at sea. "Begin, and somewhat loudly sweep the string." If you have a talent, says Milton, and are asked to use it in the service of your friend, do not be coy, do not wait to be teased; do it with all your might and as well as you can. If the situation had been reversed, you would have wanted your friend to sing for you:

> So may some gentle Muse
> With lucky words (words of good auspices) favor my
>   destined urn,
> And as he passes turn,
> And bid fair peace be to my sable shroud.

(ll. 19-22)

So far we have had an introduction or prologue in the classical manner, stating the situation, setting the mood. Now we come to the first of the three main sections into which *Lycidas* is divided. (In spite of identation and punctuation, I prefer to begin Part I with lines 23-24.)

> For we were nursed upon the self-same hill,
> Fed the same flock, by fountain, shade, and rill.

So, indeed, the two shepherds had grown up together on the hill of learning at Cambridge. In those days when the curriculum was prescribed and not elective, two students at Christ's College did many things together.

Together both, ere the high lawns appeared
Under the opening eyelids of the morn,
We drove afield.

(ll. 25-27)

At Cambridge, students began the day at five o'clock with morning
prayers and services, went to breakfast at six, and to classes at
seven. They were together in the morning, at high noon ("What
time the gray-fly winds her sultry horn") throughout the afternoon
and into the evening, when Hesperus, the evening star rose. Since
King, like Milton, had been an unusually serious student, they had
both studied—perhaps together—far later into the night than the
regulations required or—indeed—permitted: a serious matter in
days when artificial lighting was primitive and, as Milton's case
proved, hard on student eyes.

But it had not all been hard work at Cambridge, even for these
two young men who studied later and longer than classmates.
There had been plenty of extra-curricular activities. As in *L'Allegro* there was singing and dancing ("the rural ditties were not
mute"). Then as now there were various kinds of dancers. Students—particularly girls—will catch the sly humor of the "rough
Satyrs" and "Fauns with cloven heel," if they know what satyrs and
fauns looked like and what they represented. "And old Damoetas
loved to hear our song." Many years ago in my salad days, I was
sure I knew who "old Damoetas" was, and wrote an article to
identify him with Joseph Mede, the great Biblical scholar, one of
the most learned men at Cambridge, but also immensely popular
with undergraduates to whom he often gave affectionate and teas-
ing nick-names. There have been other claimants since that time.
It does not matter: Some "member of the faculty," as we would
say, who used to share the evening pleasures of his students.

So far the first part has been happy reminiscence of days and
evenings at college, almost as light in mood as *L'Allegro*. Remembering the pleasure of happy times together, we forget for a
moment what has happened, until our ears, attuned to the "glad
sound" hear a different note:

> But Ō the hēavy chańge, now thōu art gōne,
> Now thōu art gōne, and nēver mūst retūrn!
>
> (ll. 37-38)

Read the words aloud. You should always read Milton aloud and let your ears listen, for he is one of the greatest poets of sound. The spondaic emphasis is the tolling of a bell, cutting across happy memories with the insistent reiteration: "But he is dead." Like the Sicilian poets, Milton phrases his "lament of Nature." The woods and caves are silent, no longer echoing to the young voice that once sang there. The willows and the hazels will never again fan their joyous leaves to the sound of his voice. His death is reflected in the death of many things in Nature. The comparisons are to blights that cause the death of young things. As the disease of canker kills the rose, as the worm kills the young herds and flocks, as frost kills flowers, so ugly death has killed the promise of youth.

Why did God let it happen? (ll. 50-63) It is the rebellious cry of every generation, even though still couched in pagan pastoral language. Edward King was drowned. Where were the nymphs, the guardians of the waves? Either they should have been on the water or, if on land, where they could watch the water. Since King had been drowned in the Irish Channel, Milton calls to the nymphs in places associated with the western coast of the British Isles: Mona (Anglesey), an island off the Welsh coast, hills sacred to the Druids, the river Dee—a water-image—"wizard" because of legends that the motion of the waters of that river prognosticated future events. "If only," as we have all said regretfully, "if only." But we speak in vain. "Ay, me, I fondly (foolishly) dream." If only the nymphs had been there. The mood deepens as the poet remembers another young singer, far more important than this one, who met a sudden death: Orpheus. Here is that recurrent motif we have already found in *L'Allegro* and *Il Penseroso,* but in very different strain. This is not the love story of Orpheus and Eurydice. The founder of music and poetry, who could charm stones and trees and wild animals with his lyre, was killed by enraged Bacchantes whose rites he had dared watch, torn to pieces, and his dismembered body thrown into the Hebrus River—a water-image:

> His gory visage down the stream was sent,
> Down the swift Hebrus to the Lesbian shore.
>
> (ll. 62-63)

Such was the fate of the father of poetry, himself the son of a Muse, Calliope, who was powerless to save her son.

The mood has deepened and become increasingly sombre, as Milton's subconscious reflections upon his own life become more and more involved with the life and death of his subject. The death of youth is always shocking, and accidental death most unbearable of all. Milton's mother had died shortly before he wrote this poem, but she had died in the fullness of years, having lived a good life. Milton and King had been almost the same age. Like young people of all times they had felt that "The World was all before them, where to choose." Suddenly one was dead, by shipwreck. Milton was about to take ship for Italy. The parallels were very close between two young men who had devoted themselves to study and to poetry at Cambridge. "Cui bono?"

> Alas! what boots it with uncessant care,
> To tend the homely slighted shepherd's trade,
> And strictly meditate the thankless Muse?
>
> (ll. 64-66)

Perhaps our classmates were wiser than we, with their easy hedonistic philosophy of "carpe diem." While we studied late at night, they sported with Amaryllis and Neaera—lovely names for charming girls. What were we working for, King and I? Was it for fame, that spur that leads men "to scorn delights and live laborious days?" (ll. 70-72) The desire for fame may be an infirmity, but if so, it is the last from which even noble minds free themselves. (The parenthetical line is almost a direct quotation from Tacitus.) But what *is* fame? At the very moment that we reach out eager hands for reward, expecting a blaze of glory

Comes the blind Fury with the abhorréd shears,
And slits the thin-spun life.

(ll. 75-76)

This is an extraordinary figure, so pregnant with meaning that many critics miss its full portent. The shears that cut the thread of life belonged to the Fates; Clotho spun, Lachesis carded, Atropos cut the thread when the time had come. We think of the Fates as some of us have seen them among the Elgin Marbles in the British Museum, much like the presiding spirit of *Il Penseroso* who could forget herself to marble, calm and just, with an immense passivity. What has Milton done? He has deliberately transferred the scissors of the Fates to one of a very different trio—the Furies. They also were three in number, but their function was quite different. Avenging deities, they sought a culprit throughout the world and found him, bringing vengeance upon him. But Milton has done still more with his figure. In pictorial art, the Furies have the brightest and most searching of eyes—which they need to find their prey. Milton has blinded the eyes of the Fury to whom he has given the shears. Life and death—it is all as meaningless as that. We have reached the nadir of Part I.

But across the sombre pessimism, another note strikes on our ears. It begins abruptly in the middle of a line.

"But not the praise,"
Phoebus replied, and touched my trembling ears.

(ll. 76-77)

There is a reminiscence here of a Virgilian eclogue in which Apollo touched the poet's ears, bidding him not be impatient for ambition. The fame of sudden blaze is only Fama, rumor, that flies over the housetops, a false glitter. True fame is not pagan but Christian; God, who alone can pronounce upon each life, says, "Well done, thou good and faithful servant. . . . Enter thou into the joy of thy lord." The first part of *Lycidas* is over. From patterns that any classical writer might have used, we have imperceptibly risen from paganism to Christianity*

Part II begins on conventional pastoral strain, again with an introduction:

> O fountain Arethuse, and thou honored flood,
> Smooth-sliding Mincius, crowned with vocal reeds,
> That strain I heard was of a higher mood.
> But now my oat proceeds. . . .
>
> (ll. 85-88)

The two water-images imply the two sources of pastoral elegy. Arethusa, who to escape Alpheus, was turned into a fountain, was in Sicily, home of Theocritus, Bion, Moschus. The reedy river Mincius was associated with Virgil's Eclogues. Milton is saying in effect: "Oh, spirit of pastoral poetry, I have risen to the higher strains of Christianity, but now I return to the pagan conventions of the pastoral elegy, and again sing my shepherd's song." Yet there is a subtle change here, which we shall find as Part II develops. In the classical tradition, the "shepherd" was a poet. But the word "shepherd" had a different connotation to the Christian. Edward King had written poetry at Cambridge, but primarily he had been preparing himself for holy orders. To the Christian, Christ was the Good Shepherd, who gave His life for His sheep. Watch

---

* Here, it will be seen, I disagree with those critics who hold that Part I is pagan, Part II, Christian. For example, M. H. Abrams says, "Five Types of *Lycidas*" (in *Milton's Lycidas: the Tradition and the Poem*), pp. 227-228: "The immediate comfort is vouchsafed the singer in a thought in which the highest pagan ethics comes closest to the Christian: the distinction between mere earthly reputation and the need of true fame awarded by a divine and infallible judge. The concept is only tangentially Christian, however, for the deities named in this passage, Phoebus and Jove, are pagan ones." Here I cannot agree. "Pan" and "Christ," "Jove" and "God" are used interchangeably by Milton as by most Renaissance poets. Milton was too good a classicist to give the epithet "all-judging" to the wrong deity. Jove was not the judge of Hades; Rhadamanthus was. And Milton himself, as Mr. Abrams notes, indicates that the strain he has just heard was of a "higher mood," just as in the Prologue to Book IX of *Paradise Lost* and elsewhere, he emphasizes the "higher argument" of a Christian epic over a pagan.

and see how imperceptibly we pass from one connotation to the other.

As in Part I, Milton introduced an old convention, the "lament of Nature," so here he uses another, "the procession of mourners." The first lines of Part II might have been written by any of the classical poets. Neptune, god of the sea, sends his herald, who is joined by Hippotades, god of winds, both of whom declare that there was no storm when Edward King's ship went down. Indeed, it was so calm that Panope and her sisters, the fifty daughters of Nereus, were playing on the waves. To the pagan mind, there could have been no explanation other than that the ship had been built during an eclipse, a time when omens were inauspicious, making the bark "fatal" and "rigged with curses dark."

With subtle transition Milton introduces into the conventional pagan procession, Camus—a water-image. The spirit of Cambridge is personified not as *alma mater,* since this is a masculine procession, but as a reverend sire: Cambridge was already old when Milton was young. Milton may have written impatiently to Diodati that Cambridge was no place for poets, but the spell that Cambridge casts over her sons echoes in the lovely lines in which the poet anthropomorphizes the slow little river Cam, so familiar to Cambridge undergraduates of every generation, sedge-grass growing along the banks, shadows in the water, "inwrought with figures dim," and hyacinths along the banks—Greek hyacinths, bearing upon their petals the Greek words "ai, ai" (alas) in memory of the slain youth, Hyacinthus. The spirit of Cambridge speaks only one line, but it is an epitaph any graduate might envy: " 'Ah, who hath reft,' quoth he, 'my *dearest* pledge?' "

Almost imperceptibly we have again risen above the pagan conventions. The "reverend sire" prepares us for a sire more reverend still:

Last came, and last did go
The pilot of the Galilean Lake.

(ll. 108-109)

Among the many associations he might have made with the earlier life of St. Peter, Milton inevitably chooses a water-image, remembering that he was a pilot on the Lake of Galilee. As he stands before us, the climax of the procession, he is the founder of the Church: "Thou art Peter, and upon this rock I will build my church. . . . I will give unto thee the keys of the kingdom of Heaven." Here is another recurrent motif in Milton. The "two massy keys . . . of metals twain," we shall see again in *Paradise Lost*. Upon his head St. Peter wears the Bishop's mitre. Camus had praised Edward King as an outstanding student. St. Peter eulogizes him as the true shepherd-priest who would have devoted his life to his flock. His invective is turned upon the false clergy, "our corrupted clergy, then in their height," as Milton's prose-preface put it.

While reading these lines, every student of Milton should turn to one of the finest explications ever written upon any passage of poetry, Ruskin's first essay in *Sesame and Lilies*. Word by word Ruskin analyzes this passage, showing his audience how to read a piece of poetry close-packed with meaning. The false clergy are those who enter the Church for base motives. They "creep and intrude and climb into the fold." The verbs are chosen carefully, to describe those who creep in underhand ways, those who intrude —thrust themselves—into the fold, those who get to the top by climbing over the shoulders of others. They are in the sheepfold, not to care for the sheep, but only for material gain, for what they can get out of it. They have not bothered to learn their craft. They scarcely know how to hold the instruments they are supposed to use. They eat and drink, and the songs they sing are "lean and flashy." Instead of making music, they "grate on their scrannel pipes of wretched straw." Stop and say that aloud and listen to the cacophony. It is deliberately one of the ugliest lines Milton ever wrote. And meanwhile, what of the flocks? While the shepherds eat and drink, the hungry sheep are not fed. The dread plague of sheeprot spreads among them, a fearful epidemic among sheep that are starving and dirty. Many die in the sheepfold, and for those that live there waits close by the "grim Wolf with privy paw," the Roman Catholic Church, only too ready to eat up sheep neglected by Protestant shepherds.

The bitter invective against "our corrupt clergy" has been summed up in one phrase that falls from the lips of the father of the Church: "Blind mouths." Here is one of the most famous examples of Milton's extraordinary ability to say much in little, to cross-fertilize images until they are so compressed and pregnant with meaning that they become the despair of critics who spend their ingenuity in trying to find still more cryptic meanings. Let us not stop over the many interpretations that have been made of this apparently mixed metaphor. Ruskin was right beyond question, I believe, because he understood better than those who preceded and many who have followed, the way in which Milton's allusive imagination worked.

St. Peter is a bishop. The word *bishop* and the word *Episcopal* are both derived from a Greek word (episkopeo) which means "one who oversees." The function of the Bishop is to watch over his flock. The worst thing that could happen to a bishop is that he should be blind. The word *pastor* is derived from a Latin word meaning "to pasture" or "to feed." Starvation will come upon the flock if the pastor who should feed his sheep becomes a mouth. Here, as in a lightning flash, is the supreme invective of the founder of the Church upon "blind bishops and greedy pastors."

A still more mysterious crux occurs in the last two lines of Part II. Having inveighed against false bishops and pastors, St. Peter prophesies their doom:

'But that two-handed engine at the door
Stands ready to smite once, and smite no more.'

(ll. 130-131)

"Engine" might refer to almost any instrument. "Engines of destruction" was a familiar phrase in Milton's time. I shall make no attempt to summarize the fifty interpretations that have been offered for "that two-handed engine," ranging from a suggestion that

E

it refers to the two Houses of Parliament to a most ingenious theory of a Columbia University student in a Master's essay (published in part by Claude Thompson, " 'That Two-Handed Engine' will Smite") that the "engine" might be the kind of mechanical clock familiar in Milton's day. In the tower of old St. Paul's, for example, was one in which the arm of an angel pointed warningly to the hour that marked the passage of time, ready to strike with two hands the hour of one. If we must visualize the engine of destruction, I think we may best do so as the great sword which the Archangel Michael brought down "with huge two-handed sway" upon Satan in *Paradise Lost* (VI. 251). Personally, I do not think that Milton visualized it, nor did he intend us to. He did not know how judgment was to come upon the corrupt clergy; he was assured only that fearful justice would be meted out to them, prophesied by the voice of doom, saying: "Vengeance is mine, I will repay, saith the Lord." The second part of *Lycidas* is over.

As at the conclusion of Part I, we have again risen from pagan convention to Christianity, though the voice we have heard is that of the Old Testament rather than the New, a "dread voice," as Milton says. We return to the classical tradition and conventions, again through a water-image, the river Alpheus, which takes us back to the "fountain Arethuse" of Part I, since in mythology the hunter-god Alpheus pursued the nymph Arethusa under the sea to Sicily, where Arethusa had become a fountain, whose waters finally mingled with his. Again, the figure implies both Sicily and Italy. Theocritus and Virgil. As in the two previous parts, Milton introduces another convention, this time the passage of flowers, brought to strew "the laureate hearse where Lycid lies." (An interesting interpretation of this and the following passage will be found in Wayne Shumaker, "Flowerets and Sounding Seas," in *Milton's Lycidas: The Tradition and the Poem,* pp. 125-135.) There are reminiscences in Milton's flower-passage of Shakespeare's in *The Winter's Tale,* though Milton naturally emphasizes flowers that seem to mourn: "every flower that sad embroidery wears"; "the rathe primrose that forsaken dies"; "the pansy freaked with jet."

The amaranth sheds its beauty, the cowslips hang their pensive heads, and "daffadillies fill their cups with tears." Again, as in Part I, death in Nature reflects the death of a shepherd.

Across the old convention, as in the tolling of the line in Part I, "But O the heavy change now thou art gone," comes the poignant realization that even the last sad rites of decking the laureate hearse are denied the mourners. The body of Lycidas is lost and will never be found. The water-theme reaches its height in the lines beginning:

> Ay me! whilst thee the shores and sounding seas
> Wash far away, where'er thy bones are hurled.
>
> (ll. 154-155)

The great power of the passage is as overwhelming as the "whelming tide," that relentlessly carries us with it, as it dispassionately and with fearful impersonality, carries the flotsam and jetsam the sea sucks down or casts up—timber of wrecked ships, floating or engulfed bodies of the drowned. "Where'er thy bones are hurled" —our imaginations sweep in a long journey around the British Isles, from the farthest outposts of the "stormy Hebrides," the remote northwestern islands, then to the "bottom of the monstrous world," inhabited only by mysterious sea-monsters, then round the coast, under the Irish Sea, to the southwest corner of England, Land's End, in Roman times called "Bellerium," after the giant Bellerus. Here St. Michael's Mount guards the shore. As in a vision our imaginations are swept again along the southern shore to Spain, "Namancos and Bayona's hold," toward which the Archangel Michael, "the great Vision of the guarded mount" seems to look. Northwest, southwest, south or east—we shall never know on what far-flung journey the lonely body of our dead friend has been carried:

> Look homeward, Angel, now and melt with ruth,
> And O ye dolphins, waft the hapless youth.
>
> (ll. 163-164)

Christian archangel, classical dolphins who in legend carried the living Arion safe to shore, brought to shore, too, the dead body of Palaemon. Pagan and Christian, death and life, the two strains combine in the triumphant conclusion in which they are inextricably conjoined.

> Weep no more, woeful shepherds, weep no more,
> For Lycidas, your sorrow, is not dead.
>
> (ll. 165-166)

So pagan might have said, so Christian, though they couched the belief in different images. The pagan might use the analogy of the sun setting and rising: at night, the sun seems to disappear into the ocean, but in the morning, with renewed radiance, it "flames in the forehead of the morning sky." The Christian thinks of the Resurrection through Christ. Of the many aspects in which he might have remembered Christ, Milton inevitably chooses a water-image: Christ walking upon the waves that threatened His disciples, "the dear might of him that walked the waves." The pagan shepherd has left this world for the groves and streams and nectar of the Isles of the Blest. The Christian soul has ascended into Heaven, where, as in Revelation, he hears the inexpressible "nuptial song," the marriage supper of the Lamb. As in Dante's *Paradiso,* he enters into the communion of saints,

> In solemn troops and sweet societies
> That sing, and singing in their glory move,
> And wipe the tears forever from his eyes.
>
> (ll. 179-181)

We hear the echo of Revelation VII. 17, when "the Lamb shall be their shepherd . . . and God shall wipe away every tear from their eyes."

As we began with a pagan convention, so we end, as the shepherds cease their lament. Drowned though he was, their friend has not died in vain. He has become the Genius, the tutelary deity of the shore of the sea that claimed his body but left free his spirit to guide and protect those who come after. Pagan and Christian combine for all of us must "wander in that perilous flood," the dangers of the world each of us must encounter on our journey through life.

The song of the shepherd, with its antiphonal mourning and triumph, is over. Like various of his classical predecessors, Milton adds an epilogue, in which the first person changes to the third: "Thus sang the uncouth swain to the oaks and rills." So an unknown shepherd has sung his pastoral elegy in memory of a dead friend. But the day is over. The sun has stretched out all the hills and dropped into the western bay. It is time to take home the sheep. Life must go on in spite of death. Tomorrow he will lead his flock again, but to another pasture in which there will be fewer memories and echoes of a dead friend. The shepherd's song for Lycidas is over.

Structure of *Lycidas*

I have said that we must read *Lycidas* together twice, once for careful analysis, again for synthesis, and so we shall. But before I turn to synthesis, I must stop over peculiarities of the structure and style of the poem which make it unique in English—or, indeed, any other—poetry. Faithful though it is in many ways to the classical conventions, *Lycidas* is like no preceding classical or Renaissance elegy, as it is unlike the later *Adonais* or *Thyrsis*. It follows no stanzaic pattern known among classical or English poets. Indeed, we usually speak of it as a succession of "verse paragraphs," rather than stanzas. There are eleven of these, in length from ten to thirty-one lines. Some lines rhyme, but in no regular pattern. Ten lines, scattered at irregular intervals, do not rhyme at all. The metre is basically iambic pentameter, but fourteen lines are trimeter, which are always rhymed and always with pentameter lines, not with each other. Only the Epilogue is in a regular form, *ottava rima*. The structure of the whole poem, as I have showed you in my analysis, is tripartite, with an introduction and epilogue, but again there is no regularity in the lengths of the parts. Part I (as I have read it) is sixty-one lines; Part II, forty-six; Part III, fifty-three lines.

Conscious as he always was of models, did Milton have a pattern for his extraordinary non-stanzaic stanza form? Many suggestions have been made, though no two critics tend to agree with one another. Each has his favorite hypothesis, or, indeed, lets his imagination play with several, as I shall let mine. In his juvenilia, we watched Milton experimenting with stanzaic pattern and setting himself metrical exercises. On two occasions, in "On Time" and "At a Solemn Music," we caught anticipations of *Lycidas*. I said at that time that Milton might have been attempting a variant upon the Pindaric Ode. If I were to suggest that Part III of *Lycidas* (and to some extent, Part II) consists of strophe (the flower-passage), antistrophe (the "sounding sea") and epode (the apotheosis) I should be using the terms not as Pindar would have used them, to be sure, but hardly more loosely than did many who thought themselves his followers. But I shall not attempt to prove that *Lycidas* is a series of Pindaric odes. Nor shall I develop another hypothesis which sometimes teases me: similarities between *Lycidas* and the *genre* of the "meditation" (what Louis Martz calls "the poetry of meditation") or the kind of devotional literature we find in John Donne's prose-poem *Devotions,* each of which falls into three parts, Meditation, Expostulation, Prayer. (The "fame" passage and that of St. Peter might prove nice examples of "expostulation" and each of the three parts of *Lycidas* rises to religious climax.) But again the passing similarities are too vague to offer any real explanation for the extraordinarily subtle structure of *Lycidas.*

If Milton was following any literary tradition, I incline to that suggested by W. P. Ker and most fully and persuasively developed by F. T. Prince ("The Italian Element in *Lycidas,"* in *Milton's Lycidas: The Tradition and the Poem,* pp. 153-166). Mr. Ker said: "You cannot fully understand Lycidas without going back to Italy and the theory and practice of the *canzone."* He believed that the "solemn odes" written in England from Spenser's *Epithalamion* down to the nineteenth century stemmed from Dante's description of the *canzone* in *De Vulgari Eloquentia*. I refer you to Mr. Prince for a much fuller explanation, quoting from him only a few passages which may explain to you what *canzone* implies.

> A *canzone* consisted of a complex, fully rhymed stanza of some length, repeated several times and followed by a shorter concluding stanza, the *commiato*. . . . The stanza of a *canzone* is most commonly built of two sections, which are linked by a key line or *chiave*. Such a stanza was called a *stanza divisa*. . . . The first part of a *stanza divisa* must be linked to the second by a line rhyming with the last line of the first; this line was the *chiave* or key.

In Italy had come about a liberation of lyric verse from such over-rigid stanzaic form, a liberation with which Milton was undoubtedly familiar, particularly in Tasso's *Aminta* and Guarini's *Il Pastor Fido*, marked by irregular lyric and partially rhymed semi-lyrical passages, which are similar in various ways to *Lycidas*. So much for various literary traditions which may or may not lie behind the poem. I have been careful to say, "If Milton was following a literary tradition." But was the model or pattern of *Lycidas* primarily literary, or may he have been deliberately attempting a wedding of two "sister arts," poetry and music?

Lycidas—A Synthesis

When such earlier critics as George Saintsbury, J. H. Hanford, Laurence Binyon and a number of others were writing of *Lycidas*, musical analogies were often on their lips. The effect of the poem was "symphonic," its changing moods were "changing keys"; the pleasure it produces is the pleasure of music. At least as early as 1924, somewhat younger than these elder statesmen, I too was teaching *Lycidas* by musical analogies, and like them using such terms as "symphony" and "sonata." I knew these parallels were anachronistic, for Milton would not have understood these terms as we use them in the twentieth century, but I had no musical vocabulary contemporary with Milton's, nor did I know what musical forms he might have known. It remained for one of my student-colleagues at Smith College to tell me what I had only vaguely surmised, that there *were* musical forms familiar to Milton, resembling closely the structure and style of *Lycidas*. In Gretchen Finney's "A Musical Background for *Lycidas*" (*Musical Backgrounds for English Literature,* pp. 194-219), you will find the vocabulary and the background I lacked, and will learn how close *Lycidas* is to certain forms of Italian music contemporary with Milton. She will explain, too, why Milton wrote in the prose-preface: "In this monody the author bewails a learned friend." *Monody* is a term with both literary and musical connotations. In literature it is usually associated with a poem of lament sung by one person for another. It denoted as well a musical style, supposed to have been used in Greek tragedy. In Italy in Milton's time the word *monodia,* as Mrs. Finney says, "was used specifically for music sung by a solo voice in the new recitative style. . . . Monody was discussed usually in connection with musical drama." *Lycidas* is a monody in both the literary and musical senses. Let us read it again to see how Milton united two arts.

Lycidas begins with an introduction which is also an overture to a piece of music, a kind of oratorio, in which Milton sets two dominant motifs, which will echo antiphonally, now in apparent opposition, now one transcending the other. They are embodied for me in the "laurel" and the "myrtle" the poet plucks in classical fashion to symbolize the "melodious tear" shed by the mourner that the soul of his dead shepherd-friend might find rest. Myrtle and laurel, sadness and triumph—let your ears listen for them, and do not forget that the laurel is mentioned first, as it will be sounded last.

From the overture, we come to Part I, the first movement of my anachronistic "sonata-symphony." It begins in pastoral strain, with the simple music of the shepherd's pipes and a solo voice:

For we were nursed upon the self-same hill,
Fed the same flock by fountain, shade, and rill.

(ll. 23-24)

Simple, quiet, almost prosaic in diction, the lines introduce a passage of conventional pastoral elegy in which the voice of the shepherd tells of long leisurely days spent by two young shepherds on the hill of learning. Rising before daylight, together "ere the high lawns appeared under the opening eyelids of the morn," they "drove afield" until high noon, then into the afternoon and often far into the night, studying while others slept or sported with Amaryllis. But it was not all hard work at Cambridge:

Meanwhile the rural ditties were not mute,
Tempered to the oaten flute,
Rough Satyrs danced and Fauns with cloven heel
From the glad sound would not be absent long.

(ll. 25-32)

There is a change in the music; they dance to the glad sound, the Fauns as light and gay as the dancers in *L'Allegro,* the Satyrs, grotesquely amusing, rather like Comus' rabble rout. The pastoral music of the dance makes us remember only happy days and evenings at Cambridge and forget for a moment that they will not come again.

Across the pastoral fields, as across the dancing music, comes the ominous tolling of the passing bell:

But Ō, the hēavy chānge, nōw thōu art gōne,
Now thōu art gōne, and nēver mūst retūrn!

The mood begins to deepen as the myrtle motif emerges in the lament of Nature for a dead shepherd—canker, taint-worm, frost, ugly names for ugly powers that kill the young in Nature. The myrtle motif deepens still more as the shepherd who is left cries aloud: "Why did the gods—why did God—permit this to happen?" Reflection upon the meaninglessness of life grows more sombre as the poet remembers the death not only of another unknown young poet but of the father of poetry, Orpheus, greatest of them all,

E*

torn to pieces by enraged and intoxicated Bacchantes. The music is strident, cacophonous as the furious "rout that made the hideous roar," as the dismembered body of Orpheus was carried by the relentless stream "down the swift Hebrus to the Lesbian shore."

If this is all there is to life, what does anything mean? Why did we labor those long days and nights, Edward King and I? If it was for fame, what then is fame?

> Were it not better done as others use,
> To sport with Amaryllis in the shade,
> Or with the tangles of Neaera's hair?
>
> (ll. 67-69)

Lines which against their somber setting, catch for the moment the Cavalier music of *carpe diem*. Life has not only meaning but tragic irony, for at that moment when we hold out eager hands for the "fair guerdon" and "think to burst out into sudden blaze,"

> Comes the blind Fury with the abhorred shears,
> And slits the thin-spun life.
>
> (ll. 75-76)

Now that you understand the closely-packed figure, you see how horrible it is, a symbol of the blind, perverse meaninglessness of life in which there is no design, no plan, no justice, no God— only blind Fury. This is both the height and the nadir of the myrtle motif.

But across man's questioning of God and the despair that can find no meaning in the universe, abruptly—in the middle of a line —we hear the laurel replying to the myrtle, the beginning of triumph:

> "But not the praise,"
> Phoebus replied, and touched my trembling ears.
>
> (ll. 76-77)

The "fame" you sought was not true fame. Fame is no plant of mortal soil, no guerdon of flashy tinsel, no "sudden blaze" of a moment's adulation from your fellow-men. True fame is in the sight of God. There *is* justice, there *is* meaning, there *is* reward in the "pure eyes And perfect witness of all-judging Jove," who alone can say: "Well done, thou good and faithful servant; enter now into the joy of thy reward." The laurel motif rises to a crescendo as the Divine Voice seems accompanied by a chorus of angels, welcoming the true and faithful shepherd into the joys of Paradise. The first movement of *Lycidas* is over. Instrumental accompaniment, solo voice and choral come to a climax in the "higher mood" as the laurel of Christianity triumphs over the myrtle of lament.

The second movement, like the first, begins with pastoral strain as the shepherd's "oat proceeds," and he introduces the procession of mourners, the Herald of the Sea, Hippotades, Camus. The first movement was secular, devoted to the "shepherd as poet." This is ecclesiastical, a lament for the "shepherd as priest." The spirit of Cambridge, in his one solo line, praises the son he had trained for the priesthood: "Ah, who hath reft," quoth he, "my dearest pledge?" The music deepens as St. Peter (a basso profundo, I feel sure) inveighs against the false clergy who "creep and intrude and climb" into the fold for material gain. The invective rises to a first climax of sound in the passion of that terrible phrase, "Blind mouths!" Deliberate cacophony cuts across the harmony in phrase after phrase of ugly words: "for their bellies's sake"; "how to scramble at the shearers' feast"; "swoln with wind and the rank mist," most of all in the discordant sound as

> lean and flashy songs
> Grate on their scrannel pipes of wretched straw.
> (ll. 123-124)

The myrtle motif has remained dominant throughout the second movement. Although the rest of the movement has been recitative, the last two "laurel" lines:

> But that two-handed engine at the door
> Stands ready to smite once, and smite no more
> (ll. 130-131)

are—in my ears—choral. Other singers join with the voice of St. Peter as orchestra and the full chorus of "ancestral voices prophesying" rise to a great crescendo. How and when judgment will come, we do not know, but come it will: "Vengeance is mine and recompense." "I will repay," saith the Lord. As in Revelation "there followed silence in Heaven."

The third movement, like the first and second, begins in pastoral strain, with inherited conventions. The "lament of Nature," the "procession of mourners" is paralleled by the "catalogue of flowers," mourning the dead shepherd. This passage might well be choral. The tempo is deliberately slowed in the last line:

To strēw the laūreate heārse where Lȳcid līes (1.151).

Recitative begins in the passage, "Ay me!" but this is the declamatory, the oratorical style. "One is impressed," as Mrs. Finney says, "by its grandiloquence, the loud, open vowels, the prolonged quantity of the words"—all add to that sense of vast distance, remoteness, loneliness as our imaginations are carried with the drowned body from northwest to south, from south across the Channel to Spain, returning again to England with the "great Vision of the guarded mount." We feel the destructive power of impersonal Nature in the "sounding seas" that "wash far away," in the violence of, "where'er thy bones are hurled," the "stormy Hebrides," the "whelming tide," the "bottom of the monstrous world." Across the myrtle of lament not only for death but for the destruction of the body begins to rise the laurel motif, as we hear a Christian promise of Heaven in "Look homeward, Angel," a pagan memory of the salvation of a body by dolphins.

The laurel rises to its climax in the great choral passage in which all voices combine in victorious crescendo:

> Weep no more, woeful shepherds, weep no more,
> For Lycidas, your sorrow, is not dead.
>
> (ll. 165-166)

The pagan expressed the belief in natural terms—much like those of Ecclesiastes, the Preacher—"The sun also riseth, and the sun

goeth down and hasteth to the place where it riseth." The theme
of the rebirth and renewal in Nature rises with the sun to that glorious line:

> Flames in the forehead of the morning sky.
>
> (1. 171)

So too the Christian strain of the mighty chorus soars as the soul
of the dead shepherd-priest rises to the "solemn troops and sweet
societies" of the saints in Paradise, reaching a climax in the majestic lines:

> That sing, and singing in their glory move,
> And wipe the tears forever from his eyes.
>
> (ll. 180-181)

The rebirth of Nature, the Resurrection of the soul "through the
dear might of him that walked the waves"—for pagan and for
Christian lament and mourning have given way to rejoicing. Life
has triumphed over death. Immortality has overcome mortality.
There *is* meaning, there *is* justice, there *is* reward. A shepherd has
died, a body has been lost at sea, but both body and soul have
risen to immortality. The triumph of laurel over myrtle is complete.

One of the most curious misreadings of a great poem was that
of various critics (largely of the nineteenth century) who spoke of
the "fame" passage in Part I and the "St. Peter passage" in Part II
of *Lycidas* as "digressions." With his mastery of form, his architectonic sense, how could or would Milton have "digressed" in two
of the longer passages in a poem of less than two hundred lines?
Read as the poem should be read, we know that, far from being
"digressions," these are the musical, the literary, and the religious
climaxes of their movements. There are no digressions in *Lycidas,*
the most perfect long short poem in the English language.

II

THE MIDDLE YEARS

The Making
of a Statesman

The second stage of Milton's life was the "prose period," during which he poured forth hundreds of pages of polemic prose, much of it written to order, and, as he himself said, "with the left hand." If we scan the twenty volumes into which the *Columbia Milton,* still the standard edition, is divided, we see that only four volumes are devoted to poetry, sixteen to prose—an imbalance found in no other great writer who considered himself primarily a poet. Since the subject of this volume is Milton's poetry, I shall treat the prose, not for itself, but only for the light it throws upon Milton's poetic development, in which some of it is of great importance.

The Italian Journey

We left Milton at Horton, composing *Lycidas,* about to set out to "fresh woods and pastures new." His own statement about his travels, written much later in the *Second Defense of the English People,* begins (in translation): "I then became anxious to visit foreign parts, and particularly Italy. My father gave me his permission, and I left home with one servant. On my departure, the celebrated Henry Wotton, who had long been King James's ambassador at Venice, gave me a signal proof of his regard, in an elegant letter which he wrote, breathing not only the warmest friendship, but containing some maxims of conduct which I found very useful in my travels." The Grand Tour (not yet so called) was not as common in Milton's time as it became after the Restoration, but many gentlemen's sons, like Milton, considered such travel the climax of a liberal education.

Of Milton's short stay in Paris, almost no record remains. We know from his own statement that he carried a letter to Thomas Scudamore, ambassador to the King, and that through him he was introduced to Hugo Grotius, ambassador from the Queen of Sweden to the French court. Grotius was not only a diplomat; he was one of the greatest jurists of all time, whose *De Jure Belli et Pacis* (1625) marked a milestone in the history of legal concepts. Perhaps even more important in the mind of the young English Protestant, Grotius at this time was endeavoring to bring about a union of Protestants, among the churches of Sweden, Denmark, Norway and England.

If Milton crossed the Alps on horseback, as most travelers did, he left no comment upon the experience. His own detail begins when he took ship at Nice for Genoa, and found himself at last on the soil which had long been his spiritual home. From Genoa, he proceeded through Leghorn and Pisa to Florence where he settled for about two months, from there to Siena and to Rome for another two months, then south to Naples, where his meeting with John Baptista Manso, marquis of Villa, a poet and the friend of poets particularly of Tasso—marked the literary climax of his journey.

A cultivated young man of good background and attractive personality, who carried letters from such an important personage as Sir Henry Wotton, would have found many doors open to him in Italy. We know from his nephew and others that Milton was welcomed to various "academies" (those originals of our "learned societies," and our academies of arts and letters), that his poetry was praised and that poems of tribute were written to him. In addition to the formal documents he mentioned, Milton would of course have had with him more personal letters, particularly from the Diodatis and probably other foreign families established in England, which would have opened still other doors. We know that he came into contact with various musicians. Milton preserved three Latin poems, "To Leonora Singing in Rome," written to Leonora Baroni, whom he probably heard at the Barberini Palace in the autumn of 1638. Our ears will catch many memories of Italian music in both *Paradise Lost* and *Samson Agonistes.*

Originally Milton had planned to continue his travels to Sicily and Greece, but while he was still at Naples, word reached him that clouds were gathering in England. His own words in the *Second Defense* are: "When I was preparing to pass over into Sicily and Greece, the melancholy intelligence which I received of the civil commotions in England made me alter my purpose; for I thought it base to be travelling for amusement abroad, while my fellow-citizens were fighting for liberty at home." He therefore reversed his steps and made his way back to the north. The return journey was less carefree than his travels to the south. "While I was on my way back to Rome," he wrote in the *Second Defense,* "some merchants informed me that the English Jesuits had formed a plot against me if I returned to Rome, because I had spoken too freely on religion." Return to Rome he did, however, where "I again openly defended, as I had done before, the reformed religion in the very metropolis of popery." From Rome back to Florence, with a short excursus to Lucca, the original home of the Diodatis, then across the Apennines, through Bologna and Ferrara to Venice. His route then took him across Lake Geneva to Geneva, where he spent some time with Giovanni Diodati, uncle of his friend, distinguished as translator of the Bible into Italian. And so to France, from which he returned to England in August 1639.

Milton's Italian journey looks before and after. When he left England, he undoubtedly felt that this was the climactic chapter in "The Education of a Poet." But we shall see that during the fifteen months of travel, his imagination was storing up memories other than music which we shall find particularly in *Paradise Lost*. I shall not at this time pause over the Latin poem Milton wrote to Manso, except to say that it shows that he had been deliberating whether his epic (he is still sure that he is "called" to write one) was to be in Latin or English, but that he had now decided that his was to be an English *Arthuriad*.

To what extent Milton's imagination was stimulated by the paintings, murals and statuary he saw in Italy is a question that has not been answered. Some critics feel that the effect was profound and that memories of specific pictures and statues, and particularly of the Sistine Chapel, lie behind Milton's pictures of God and Satan and various scenes in *Paradise Lost*. I shall return later to consider the possibility that Milton drew his graphic picture of the "first Hell" in *Paradise Lost*—the burning lake and burning shores in Book I—from a visit to the strange volcanic district of the Phlegraean Fields near Naples, and that when he constructed his "second Hell" of Pandemonium, his memory returned to St. Peter's in Rome.

There is another problem of a different sort in connection with the Italian journey over which I shall pause at this point. In the *Areopagitica*, written in 1644, Milton said: "There . . . (at Florence) I found and visited the famous Galileo, grown old, a prisoner to the Inquisition, for thinking in astronomy other than the Franciscan and Dominican licensers thought." There seemed no problem here until, some years ago, a Swedish scholar, S. B. Liljegren (a modern counterpart to Alexander More, to whom Milton replied in the *Second Defense*) insisted that Milton lied in this statement and that he never visited Galileo. In my time, I have replied to Liljegren in "Milton and the Telescope." When Milton visited Italy, Galileo was living at Fiesole, near Florence, where his observatory still stands. As letters and other biographical material show, in spite of the fact that he was a prisoner, Galileo received a number of visitors. As I hope I have shown, access to him would have been no real difficulty to a young Englishman, bearing such letters as Milton had, particularly if the visit was made on Milton's trip south, rather than after the Jesuits threatened him.

An actual visit to Galileo is not essential for the point I shall later make of the influence of the Galilean "new astronomy" upon Milton's imagination. Galileo's works were widely known in England both before and after Milton's Italian journey. But the meeting between the two is one of those moments in history that has caught the imagination of many writers and artists. The most familiar English treatment is, of course, Walter Savage Landor's in one of the *Imaginary Conversations*. Another more recent one in poetry is Alfred Noyes', *Watchers of the Sky*. There are a number written in Italian, as well as various pictures, recreating the scene. It is, of course, the irony latent in the meeting that fascinates the sensitive observer. Galileo was old and blind and a prisoner for his scientific opinions; Milton, then in the early prime of life, was to write his greatest work when he was old and blind and for a time a prisoner of another sort of Inquisition, for his political and religious opinons.

Milton's return journey was clouded in another way. Just when he received the sad news that Charles Diodati was dead, he did not say. The one fact that is known is that Charles Diodati was buried in Blackfriars, London, on August 27, 1638, a few months after Milton had left England. Letters traveled slowly in those days though there was regular postal service between England and the continent. Only after his return to England did Milton write his elegy for his friend, the *Epitaphium Damonis,* companion poem to *Lycidas*. It was entirely natural that Milton should have used a more strict classical form of the pastoral elegy and that he wrote in Latin in memory of the dead friend with whom he had so long corresponded in Latin elegies and prose. The poem is the best evidence that news of his friend's death reached Milton late, filled with reminiscences of Milton's feeling that his friend would have joined in the pleasures he had been experiencing in Italy. "Ah, how often would I say, when already dark ashes possessed you, 'Now Damon is singing.' " He had intended to surprise Diodati by bringing him two exquisitely engraved cups Manso had presented to him. As he would have shared his treasured gifts, he would have confided to his friend his new-found assurance that he had been "called" to do for England what Virgil had done for Rome, and write an English epic glorifying English history in the person of King Arthur. But Milton came back to England in August 1639, his travels behind him, to find a very different situation from that he had left in many ways.

John Milton, Schoolmaster

The return to England was—even more than Milton himself was aware—the end of an unusually happy, sheltered and idyllic youth, devoted to "The Making of a Poet." With the exception of a small group of sonnets—"Alas, too few!"—the *Epitaphium Damonis* was the last poetry Milton was to write for many years. Wars and rumors of wars detained him from the *Arthuriad* which he had planned so happily in Italy. But there is still a brief period in his biography which must be considered before discussing the years spent in the service of the Commonwealth. Since I am here concerned with Milton's biography, I shall violate chronology and consider his tractate *Of Education* as if it had been written shortly after Milton's return from Italy rather than in 1644.

Both Milton and his father must have agreed that the time had at last come for Milton to settle down and begin to earn his living. The Church and the law had been dismissed. One profession, however, was open for which Milton had had the necessary preparation. He became a schoolmaster. Instead of returning to Horton, he established himself in London. His nephew, Edward Phillips, one of his two first students, wrote: "Soon after his return and visits paid to his father and other friends, he took him a lodging in St. Bride's Churchyard, at the house of one Russel, a tailor, where he first undertook the education and instruction of his sister's two sons, the younger whereof had been wholly committed to his charge and care." Edward and John Phillips were the sons of Milton's sister, Anne Phillips, and the brother of the "Fair Infant" who had died of a cough before their birth. With them—other boys joined the group later—Milton set into practice the educational theories he had drawn in and reacted against at St. Paul's and Christ's College.

The tractate *Of Education* shows that Milton had done a good deal of thinking on the subject. There is nothing novel or startling about the ideas in the tract, so far as the history of education is concerned. It is a characteristic treatise of Renaissance humanism, written at a period when a great deal of attention was being given to education. Milton dedicated it to Samuel Hartlib, who had apparently suggested that he write it, a man who wrote widely on many subjects, including education, and—more important—a friend of Johann Amos Comenius, (Komensky), a Moravian, one of the greatest educational authorities in Europe, to whom Milton may be referring in the last sentence of the first paragraph. As a result of our study of the "Pigeon of Paules" and "the Lady of Christ's," we can read between the lines and recognize some of the "abuses" Milton had felt in his own education, even at St. Paul's.

Milton shows himself a "modern" rather than an "ancient" in education and also reflects much of the dissatisfaction he had felt at Cambridge, when he inveighs against the "barbarous" methodology which, instead of beginning "with arts most easy . . . such as are most obvious to the sense," schoolmasters and college dons forced down the throats of their young charges, "the most intellective abstractions of logic and metaphysics: so that many of the students 'grow into hatred and contempt of learning,' "—a passage that seems to echo Bacon's invective in *The Advancement of Learning*. Milton was particularly severe upon the time wasted in the learning of Latin and Greek:

> We do amiss to spend seven or eight years merely in scraping together so much miserable Latin and Greek as might be learned

otherwise easily and delightfully in one year, . . . forcing the empty wits of children to compose themes, verses, and orations, which are the acts of ripest judgment, and the final work of a head filled, by long reading and observing with elegant maxims and copious invention. These are not matters to be wrung from young striplings, like blood out of the nose, or the plucking of untimely fruit.

Milton believed in what we call the "direct method" in teaching languages. It may have been possible that in a year or two, youngsters might write and speak Latin as well as "Paules Pigeons" after seven or eight. That Milton's method, whatever it was, "worked" is implied in Edward Phillips' memoir. He mentioned

the many authors both of the Latin and Greek, which through his excellent judgment and way of teaching, far above the pedantry of common public schools (where such authors are scarce ever heard of) were run over within no greater compass of time, than from ten to fifteen or sixteen years of age.

It is an impressive list of ten Latin and eleven Greek authors, both prose and poetry. Milton's students were not limited to the Latin and Greek. Like himself, they learned some Hebrew, and as he suggested most casually in the tractate, "where to it would be no impossibility to add the Chaldee and the Syrian dialect." More than one critic has said ironically that Milton's academy would have been an admirable training ground for students if they had all been young John Miltons. But it is interesting to see that Edward Phillips felt he had profited even by the Chaldee and Syriac. He wrote:

Nor did the time thus studiously employed in conquering the Greek and Latin tongues, hinder the attaining to the chief oriental languages, *viz.,* the Hebrew, Chaldee, and Syriac, so far as to go through the *Pentateuch,* or Five Books of Moses in Hebrew, to make a good entrance in the *Targum,* or Chaldee Paraphrase, and to understand several chapters of St. Matthew in the Syriac Testament.

Characteristically, Milton suggests that in addition to all the scholarly languages, his pupils will easily learn Italian "at any odd hour." One of the most delightful sentences in *Of Education* is that in which Milton tells us how he taught his students to pronounce Latin "as near as can be to the Italian, especially in the vowels. For we Englishmen, being far northerly, do not open our mouths in the cold air wide enough to grace a southern tongue, but are observed by all other nations to speak exceeding close and inward."

There is much more in the tracate over which we might stop if our interest were primarily with Milton's prose. One other sentence must be quoted. No one who reads it can forget Milton's definition, which every teacher should know by heart: "I call therefore a complete and generous education that which fits a man to perform justly, skilfully, and magnanimously all the offices, both private and public, of peace and war." It remains as true for our time as for the Renaissance. No finer definition has been written of the liberal education.

Milton's First Marriage

"About Whisuntide it was, or a little after, that he took a journey into the country; no body about him certainly knowing the reason, or that it was any more than a journey or recreation: after a month's stay, home he returns a married man, that went out a bachelor." So Edward Phillips succinctly summed up the facts of Milton's first marriage, which has torn critics and biographers asunder ever since. When did he wed Mary Powell? How long had he known her? Why did she leave him—as she did for nearly four years? What was the relation between the marriage and Milton's writing the *Divorce Tracts?* Did he actually write the first one while he was on his honeymoon? During the last few years, the "Powell problem" has been made even more acute by William Riley Parker's suggestion that Milton's last sonnet, "Methought I saw my late espoused saint," was written not about the second wife, as we have always believed, but about Mary Powell. ("Milton's Last Sonnet," *RES* 21. [1945], 235-8; see Huckabay Bibl. Nos. 767-768 for replies and a later article by Parker.)

None of the questions has been finally answered and perhaps never will be. But little by little, scholars have thrown light on some of them. There was a time when the romantic notion was widespread that Milton, off on a holiday perhaps, came by chance upon Mary Powell and fell in love at first sight. Milton was not at all incapable of falling in love at sight, as the fifth and seventh elegies suggest; the Italian sonnets suggest that he had been very much in love when he was younger. But his meeting with Mary Powell does not seem to have been as sudden as we used to think. Professor J. Milton French ("The Powell-Milton Bond,") came upon documents proving that the two families had had business associations for some years and that the elder John Milton had made a sizable loan to Mary's father, Richard Powell, a Justice of the Peace in Forresthill, Oxfordshire. The younger Milton may merely have gone to collect the interest from a family he had known for some time.

The problem of the date of the marriage still remains, and that is of particular importance in connection with the *Divorce Tracts*. Edward Phillips dates the marriage in May or June and Mary's return to her family about August first of the same year. But he does not mention the year. He merely indicates that the marriage occurred after Milton moved his school from St. Bride's Churchyard to Aldergate Street. On the basis of the little said by Edward Phillips, Masson and other biographers dated the marriage in May or June 1643, and his wife's return to her family about August 1 of the same year. This seems almost impossible so far as the *Divorce Tracts* are concerned, since the first one was published almost exactly on the date on which his wife supposedly left him. If Milton wrote it on his honeymoon, as a result of marital disillusionment, he must have written with incredible rapidity and the printer must have been far more expeditious than printers usually were or are.

We should remember that Edward Phillips not only did not give the year but that he was writing his memories of his uncle nearly fifty years later and looking back over a period when he himself was just entering his teens. He often kaleidoscoped events; he is sometimes inaccurate; and much of his memory of these early days was undoubtedly colored by family gossip and surmise which he half-heard. Probably his mother or his grandfather was entirely aware of the reason for Milton's journey into the country. We should notice, too, that Phillips himself said that the pamphlets were provoked, not by the wife's leaving but by her refusal to return. When the first tract appeared, Mary Milton would have just left London, with her husband's reluctant consent. It was weeks later that she refused to return. If, however, we date the marriage a full year earlier, as we incline to do nowadays, some problems are resolved. Milton would have been accustomed to his wife's absence. He may well, as some biographers surmise, have wished to marry again, both for normal reasons and because the master of a boarding school, however small, had need of a wife's assistance, particularly because Milton's elderly father had come to live with him, and three generations under one roof involved housekeeping problems almost insuperable for a single man.

Whether or not his wife's desertion was one of the causes for Milton's writing on divorce, it was not the only one. Until the questions of dating have been completely resolved—and even then—it is only just to remember what Milton himself said about the writing and publication of the pamphlets. A decade later in the *Second Defense,* Milton looked back on this period of his life and gave his reason for writing three different groups of works at this particular time. He began by discussing various ideas of liberty with which he and others were concerning themselves at this time:

When, therefore, I perceived that there were three species of liberty which are essential to the happiness of social life—reli-

gious, domestic, and civil; and as I had already written concerning the first, and the magistrates were strenuously active in
obtaining the third, I determined to turn my attention to the
second, or the domestic species. As this seemed to involve three
material questions, the conditions of the conjugal tie, the education of the children, and the free publication of the thoughts, I
made them objects of distinct consideration.

If we believe what Milton says here, the *Divorce Tracts* began in
his mind—however they ended—as an inevitable part of his
theory of domestic liberty; this involved freedom in marriage, the
education of children, and the freedom of men to publish their
own thoughts and read those of other men: the *Divorce Tracts,
Of Education,* and *Areopagitica.*

The problem of divorce has always been, and remains, a moot
one in England. While divorce was one of the issues on which
Henry VIII separated the Anglican from the Roman Church, divorce remained as difficult for the individual Anglican as for the
Roman Catholic. Milton was not the only Puritan who believed
that the regulations about divorce were far too rigid, though the
reception of his tracts by some of his own party, which he reports
in the sonnet on *Tetrachordon,* shows that his position was not
the prevailing one even among Puritans. No matter what relation
the tracts had to his private life, Milton's convictions were always
based upon fundamental theories and beliefs. In opposition to all
Catholics, and to many of his own party, Milton held that marriage was not a sacrament, which only the Church could dissolve. It was a contract, entered into by two people, which might be
voided for sufficient cause. This does not mean that Milton held a
low opinion of marriage. Quite the contrary, as we shall see when
he interprets the marriage of Adam and Eve in *Paradise Lost.* He
believed that marriage involved compatibility on three levels,
physical, spiritual and intellectual, and that if it did not, it had not
been a true marriage and should be set aside. Whatever his youthful attitude toward male chastity had been, Milton had grown up a
very normal man, and as his last sonnet proved, capable of deep

love for a wife. His was not the grudging justification of St. Paul, "It is better to marry than to burn," but rather the words of Genesis: "It is not good that man should be alone." Adam is his spokesman in *Paradise Lost* when he asks God for a mate; all other created things had mates; man only was alone:

> But with me
> I see not who partakes. In solitude
> What happiness? Who can enjoy alone? . . .
> Of fellowship I speak
> Such as I seek, fit to participate
> All rational delight.
>
> VIII. 364-66, 389-91

God is all-sufficient. "Not so is man," who asks "collateral love and dearest amity."

Areopagitica

Since Milton himself held that his works on domestic liberty were parts of a whole, we may discuss the *Areopagitica* at this time, rather than when it was published in 1644. It completes the trilogy. As the epigraph for his oration, Milton quoted lines from *The Suppliants* of Euripides, which begin:

> This is true liberty, when free-born men,
> Having to advise the public, may speak free.

Even as early as 1644, Milton was becoming aware that his own party could be as intolerant as those of the monarchy whom they had displaced. Shortly before the Civil War, the Star Chamber had revived and attempted to administer the law of censorship that all publications must be registered with the Stationers' Company, and approved by the Church through the Archbishop of Canterbury, the Bishop of London, or their deputies. In 1643 the Presbyterians, who now held the upper hand in Parliament, again attempted to enforce censorship. Milton himself had fallen under the ban, for in the ordinance of Parliament for licensing printing on June 14, 1623, he was mentioned by name in connection with the unlicensed publication of the *Doctrine and Discipline of Divorce.* "New Presbyter," as Milton wrote bitterly, "is but old Priest writ large." From this time on, we shall see that Milton departed more and more sharply from the extreme right-wing position of the Presbyterians and felt himself an Independent, though as time went on, even the Independents seemed to fall short of the ideals of toleration and freedom of conscience of which he was an ardent champion.

The *Areopagitica,* as has been said, is the greatest classical oration in the English language. Milton did not mean actually to deliver it, emulating the practice of the Greek orator Isocrates from whom he borrowed the title and upon whose orations he based the structure. He was following tradition in seeming to address the court on the hill of Ares, archetypal symbol of justice, while actually addressing the British Parliament. His theme is the freedom of the press, not quite what we mean today when we speak more loosely about freedom of speech. Surely this is one piece of prose that Milton did not write with his left hand. In his political tracts, Milton, like all other pamphleteers, was writing to order, spewing forth invective in answer to diatribe, slinging mud as mud was slung at him and other members of his party. In *Areopagitica,* however, as in *Lycidas, Paradise Lost, Samson Agonistes,* he was roused to the height of his artistic abilities. As in those beautifully articulated poems, Milton in his oration was following classical models, and as always transcending them in a "higher mood." Here, almost alone in his prose, we hear the "organ voice" for long periods. The *Areopagitica,* even apart from its theme and purpose, is great literature, ranking with the greatest English prose. It is filled with memorable sentences, particularly about books, many of which rightly have been carved on library walls throughout the English-speaking world:

For books are not absolutely dead things, but do contain a potency of life in them to be as active as that soul was whose progeny they are. . . . They are as lively, and as vigorously productive, as those fabulous dragon's teeth; and being sown up and down, may chance to spring up armed men. . . .

As good almost kill a man as kill a good book; who kills a man kills a reasonable creature, God's image; but he who destroys a good book, kills reason itself, kills the image of God, as it were, in the eye.

Many a man lives a burden to the earth; but a good book is the precious life-blood of a master spirit, embalmed and treasured up on purpose to a life beyond life.

There are many sentences over which a teacher finds himself pausing, remembering Milton as a teacher who had thought deeply on the problems of education and the growing-up process:

What advantage is it to be a man over it is to be a boy at school, if we have only escaped the ferula (the schoolmaster's rod) to come under the fescue (teacher's pointer, used for discipline) of an Imprimaturz? . . . And how can a man teach with authority, which is the life of teaching, how can he be a doctor in his book, as he ought to be, or else had better be silent, whenas all he teaches, all he delivers, is but under the tuition, under the correction of his patriarchal licenser? . . .

"I hate a pupil teacher, I endure not an instructor that comes to me under the wardship of an overseeing fist."

Not only individual sentences arrest us, but many figures of speech, particularly those recurrent motifs throughout Milton's works of light and darkness—the darkness of superstition, of bigotry, of false belief, the light of truth, of freedom, of reason, reflection in our world of the Fountain of Light. "We boast our light," Milton warns his countrymen, "but if we look not wisely on the sun itself, it smites us into darkness. . . ." These, with other recurrent themes and motifs, come to their climax in the great peroration which should have been spoken, whether in the Areopagus or in the Houses of Parliament. It cries to be read aloud, as does so much of Milton's writing. One feels that even the Presbyterians in the House of Commons, if they were true-born Englishmen, would have been shaken from lethargy and felt their blood stirring, if they had listened to those noble words beginning: "Lords and Commons of England, consider what nation it is whereof ye are, and whereof ye are the governors." "Methinks I see in my mind a noble and puissant nation rousing herself like a strong man after sleep, and shaking her invincible locks." As in *Lycidas,* triumph and warning combine into a whole.

As in all Milton's major works, the theme of *Aeropagitica* is liberty. Censorship has never succeeded, will never succeed, must never succeed, because it deprives man of his inalienable right to learn from books, as from other experience, the lessons he needs in order to maintain his freedom. Milton did not say with easy optimism, "Man is by nature free." *Freedom* and *liberty* were hard words, conditions hard to attain and only too easy to lose.

Controversial Pamplets

Since we are primarily concerned with Milton's poetry, I shall make no attempt to discuss—or even to list—many of the controversial pamphlets that poured from his pen between 1641 and 1660, but shall briefly consider a few that are important in his development toward his major poems. His first entrance into polemical writing was made while he was a schoolmaster in 1641, when he published *Of Reformation in England,* followed in quick succession by two other anti-episcopal tracts. In the comparative leisure of his study, Milton could write as a scholar and an historian, aloof from the pressures of the moment that were later to engage him. The first pamphlet at least reminds the reader of the young poet more than the later polemicist. These were followed during the next year by *The Reason of Church Government* and *An Apology for Smectymnuus,* both written before his marriage and before the actual outbreak of the Civil War on August 22, 1642. During the next three years, his prose was devoted to the *Divorce Tracts, Of Education* and *Areopagitica,* which in many ways look back to the earlier Milton and are still largely the work of the schoolmaster in his study. In 1645 Mary Powell returned to her husband, and to all intents and purposes Milton settled down for a short time to a normal life.

In spite of his close concern with the problems of politics and theology that were tearing his country asunder, the Milton of these years still seems more like the young man who had spent a placid and secluded youth than the later statesman, as we shall see when we read the first sonnet of the middle years, "When the Assault Was Intended to the City." Even in the year following the defeat of the Royalist forces at Naseby, Milton's main efforts were devoted to his teaching and "research," if we may use a modern term. His collected *Poems* were published in 1645, and during the next two or three years he was apparently working on his *History of Britain* and possibly on the *Christian Doctrine,* though the dating of this is extremely hypothetical.

But the apparent placidity of Milton's life was to be rudely interrupted. As we have still better reason to realize in the twentieth century, even those who are not actively drawn into war cannot remain aloof from the consequences of war.

> Yet much remains
> To conquer still; Peace hath her victories
> No less renowned than War, new foes arise. . . .

as Milton wrote in a sonnet to Cromwell. The execution of King Charles, on January 30, 1649, inevitably had a profound effect upon every English mind. In a country which had never known any government except monarchy, and in which one of "the king's two bodies" was revered as almost sacred, no matter what the second body might have been or done, the shock was profound, and the Puritans were forced to spend all their might justifying the regicide. Among the many who came to their aid was Milton, who, a

F

fortnight after the execution, published his *Tenure of Kings and Magistrates.* In March 1649, at the age of forty, Milton received and accepted appointment as Secretary for Foreign Tongues to the Council of State, and entered into full-time political life.

We have no equivalent today for Milton's position. The closest analogue in Great Britain would be a post attached to the Ministry for Foreign Affairs, in the United States to the Secretary of State. One of Milton's chief functions, as the title implies, was correspondence with heads of foreign states or with secretaries in their governments. Latin was still the one international language, although French was beginning to assume some diplomatic importance. Milton's nephew, commenting upon his uncle's importance, said: "He was courted into the service of this new commonwealth, and at last prevailed with . . . to take upon him the office of Latin secretary to the Council of State for all their letters to foreign princes and states; for they stuck to this noble and generous resolution, not to write to any, or receive answers from them, but in a language most proper to maintain a correspondence among the learned of all nations in this part of the world; scorning to carry on their affairs in the wheedling, lisping jargon of the cringing French, especially having a minister of state able to cope with the ablest any prince or state could employ, for the Latin tongue."

In addition Milton was to continue the war of words in pamphlets, some of them obviously written at the order of his superiors in the government. There is no question that Milton was enthusiastic about his appointment and fully aware of the responsibility laid upon him. Belief in those "most valiant deliverers of my native country" rings through the *Defensio pro Populo Anglicano* which he published in March, 1651. He rightly believed that he had the necessary qualifications for the appointment and he intended to use them with all his might. In the *Defensio* he wrote: "and true it is that from my very youth I had been bent extremely upon such sort of studies as inclined me if not to do great things myself at least to celebrate those who did."

We remember that Milton had planned an *Arthuriad,* in which he would have glorified England in its past and have prophesied still higher greatness in the future. By this time, he seems to have decided against it, for reasons that will be discussed later. The heavy duties he had assumed may well have made him feel that he was never to write the epic to which he had long felt "called." If he was not to do great things himself, he would at least celebrate those who did. At this crucial moment in England's history, he sincerely believed that these were the members of his party.

Remembering Milton's definition of a "generous education," we may pause for a moment over a problem which is constantly in the minds of college and university administrators and professors today. What is a "practical" education? One group insists upon the training of students in skills or trades which seem to bear specific relationship to crafts or professions in which the students may earn their living. Another group insists, as in the Renaissance, on a "liberal" education as best fitting men and women for life. Milton's education seems at first glance most "impractical." As a "Pigeon of Paules" and the "Lady of Christ's," he had had an unbalanced education, from the modern point of view. Even he himself had protested the years of drill in ancient languages, the long discipline in logic, in disputation, in rhetoric. Those years of apprenticeship in the "education of a poet" seemed remote from "life"—years in an ivory tower, or the "high lonely tower" of Il Penseroso. But ironically enough, no education could have proved more "practical" for the position to which he was called by the Commonwealth government. "A complete and generous education," he had written, is one "which fits a man to perform justly, skilfully, and magnanimously all the offices, both private and public, of peace and war." Latin was the international language and the new government needed an expert Latinist. In those days when controversy was carried on mainly through the press, and attack demanded counter-attack, the government needed a man who could write rapidly and vehemently in both Latin and English.

Milton was that man. He had already proved himself a dangerous opponent able to write effectively under pressure, to trade charge for charge. The tone of much seventeenth-century wrangling might lead a modern reader to believe that the tracts were the production of the vulgar—in all senses. Nothing could be less true. Milton's anti-episcopal treatises were answers to some of the most learned bishops of the Anglican Church, such as Bishop Joseph Hall and Bishop (later Archbishop) Ussher, one of the great scholars of the time. Among many other Puritans who had joined in the controversy was Milton's early tutor, Thomas Young. In the *Eikonoklastes,* the second pamphlet Milton wrote in his new position, he was on the most perilous ground of all, since he was writing in reply to the *Eikon Basilike,* a sort of diary supposed to have been written during the last months or even days by King Charles himself. Whatever its authorship and purposeful exaggeration, the work went far to create in the public mind the portrait of a martyred saint.

The opponent to whom Milton was called to reply a little later taxed his powers still more. Castigation of the Puritans who had put a king to death was not limited to the British Isles. The implications of that sentence were international, of ominous import in any monarchy. The prestige of the English government sank so low on the continent that British ambassadors faced insult, humiliation, even death. Cromwell's party was in grave peril when the *Defensio Regia pro Carolo I* appeared in the autumn of 1649, six months after Milton's appointment. The author was Salmasius (Claude Saumaise), a Frenchman living in Holland, recognized everywhere as one of the greatest scholars in the world. Using all the wealth of his learning, he published an eloquent tract addressed to the intellectual leaders of Europe, invoking anathema upon regicides who had dared send to the block the actual body of a king, and in doing so attempted to destroy kingship.

Here was a situation that tested even Milton's prowess and undoubtedly excited him more than any challenge he had ever met. In spite of the fact that he had long written in the international language, his audience in the past had been confined either to the little world of Academe at Cambridge, the still more private world of Diodati, at most to readers in England. Now he was called to address a European tribunal, far more formidable than the "Lords and Commons of England" to whom he had addressed *Areopagitica*. Milton was well aware of the intellectual stature of Salmasius (whom under other circumstances he would have admired greatly). In the *Defensio pro Populo Anglicano* he was speaking for himself—a scholar replying to a scholar—but he was spokesman even more "for the English people," his party now in precarious ascendancy. He analyzed his emotions as he wrote:

> I imagine myself not in the forum or on the rostra, surrounded by the people of Athens or of Rome, but about to address . . . the whole collective body of people, cities, states, and councils of the wise and eminent, through the wide expanse of an anxious and listening Europe. I seem to survey, as from a towering height, the far extended tracts of sea and land, and innumerable crowds of spectators, betraying in their looks the liveliest interest, and sensations the most congenial with my own.

Germans disdaining servitude, generous and lively French, stately valorous Spaniards—they were all before him as he wrote. There is natural human pride and awareness of his own abilities as he uses his long training in scholarship and debate to the full. He was writing in part for personal "fame," which even though "that last infirmity of noble mind," he had sought and would always seek. But more than that: he was speaking "for the English people," for that courageous group in whose great experiment in government he believed:

> Surrounded by congregated multitudes, I now imagine that, from the columns of Hercules to the Indian Ocean, I behold the nations of the earth recovering that liberty which they so long had lost; and that the people of this island . . . are disseminating the blessings of civilization and freedom among cities, kingdoms, and nations.

We may let his nephew Edward Phillips go on with the story, which he told in spicy, homely language:

Out comes in public the great kill-cow of Christendom, with his *Defensio Regis contra Populum Anglicanum;* a man so famous and cried up . . . that there could no where have been found a champion that durst lift up the pen against so formidable an adversary, had not our little English David had the courage to attempt the great French Goliath, to whom he gave such a hit in the forehead, that he presently staggered, and soon after fell.

Phillips' account of the effect of Milton's reply upon the prestige of Salmasius may have been slightly exaggerated, so far as Salmasius' death is concerned, but basically it is not far from the truth:

Immediately upon the coming out of the answer . . . he that till then had been chief minister and superintendent in the court of the learned Christina, Queen of Sweden, dwindled in esteem to that degree, that he at last vouchsafed to speak to the meanest servant. In short, he was dismissed with so cold and slighting an adieu, that after a faint dying reply, he was glad to have recourse to death, the remedy of evils and ender of controversies.

Milton's pamphlet did not actually win the war for his party; Cromwell's victories in Ireland and at Dunbar were doing that by the time the *Defensio* appeared—but he did win the Battle of the Books, and he won it at great cost. If Milton had been a soldier, he might well have given his life for his party. As it was, he gave what was almost as precious—his sight. Although his eyes had been failing for some time—he had already lost the sight of one— there is no question that his total blindness was hastened and in- deed caused by his refusal to stop his intensive work on the reply to Salmasius.

When my medical attendants clearly announced, that if I did engage in the work, it [the remaining eye] would be irreparably lost, their premonitions caused no hesitation and inspired no dismay. . . . My resolution was unshaken, though the alterna- tive was either the loss of my sight, or the desertion of my duty. . . . I resolved therefore to make the short interval of sight which was left me to enjoy, as beneficial as possible to the pub- lic interest.

The medical problems of Milton's blindness have engaged the attention of various modern writers—some of them physicians. His adversaries not unnaturally proclaimed that his blindness was a retribution of God for everything from his daring to reply to the King to his attack on Salmasius. But blindness had been coming upon Milton for several years. All the medical evidence was brought together a few years ago by Eleanor Brown in *Milton's Blindness* (pp. 16-48), a book of unusual interest in the study of Milton because it was written by a blind woman, who could understand some aspects of Milton's work we might not. Without entering into modern theories or vocabulary, we know how Milton's own physicians characterized it from a phrase in the Prologue to Light in Book III of *Paradise Lost:*

> but Thou
> Revisitest not these eyes, that roll in vain
> To find Thy piercing ray, and find no dawn:
> So thick a drop serene hath quenced their orbs,
> Or dim suffusion veiled.

The "dim suffusion" might suggest cataract, but we know from Milton's own remarks and those of his contemporaries that his eyes were not clouded in any way but remained as they had been, unusually bright. His physicians could classify it only by the phrase "drop serene," a translation of the medical term, "gutta serena," which as Miss Brown explains, was the medical term for "all blindness in which the eye retains a normal appearance."

The period immediately following his entrance into the political arena was undoubtedly the most difficult in Milton's life, as we can tell from a few remarks and many more implications in the tone of both his prose and his sonnets. In addition to his rapidly failing sight, Milton was laboring under serious ill health when he wrote the first *Defence,* "forced," as he says, "to write by piecemeal and break off every hour." In addition his domestic problems were made acute by the death of Mary Powell Milton in childbed in June 1652, a little over a year after his total blindness occurred.

She left three daughters, Anne, Mary and Deborah. We shall return to Mary Powell when we come to consider Milton's last sonnet. Milton continued to perform his duties as Secretary—with some assistance beginning in 1652—until he was relieved of his chief duties in 1655. It is still another indication of the value of a "generous education" that the successor chosen was another great poet in both English and Latin, Andrew Marvell.

During the intervening years Milton not only carried on the work for the state "to foreign princes and states," but continued to write in support of his party. The most important publication of these years is one of the greatest of Milton's prose works—second only to *Areopagitica* stylistically and surpassing the oration in some ways in mood: the *Defensio Secunda* or *Second Defence of the English People,* another chapter in the Salmasius controversy. Though embedded in earlier prose works we find passages on his life, his education, his political aspirations, adding up to what may be called his "Biographia Literaria," those in the *Second Defence* are the longest and most personal of all his biographical digressions. In style Milton rises to heights he never reached in the first *Defence.* He could be wickedly and saltily amusing. He could be simple and straightforward, plain, clear, but immensely moving, as in the account of his life. He could throw volleys of invective; he could write in the grand oratorical style, as in the panegyric on Cromwell. But as E. M. W. Tillyard points out in his excellent stylistic analysis of the *Second Defence* (*Milton,* pp. 198 ff.), the effects are particularly felt only when one reads the Latin; they are lost (or at least muted) in most English translations. Mr. Tillyard says:

By writing in a foreign tongue Milton has of necessity sacrificed the homeliness and freshness that enlivened the style of his English prose. We are remote from the language of everyday speech and frankly in the realms of rhetoric. But granted the rhetorical setting, the way Milton makes the Latin language obey him, rousing it to eloquence, subduing it to plainness, hushing it to a poetical solemnity, or goading it to the brutalities of his satire, is astonishing. He seems perfectly at ease in the sonorities of Latin and puts them, regally, to whatever use he desires.

The great English prose of *Areopagitica,* as well as some of its themes, in a way looked back to *Comus* and *Lycidas. The Second Defence,* in its mastery of styles and in its moods, looks forward to *Paradise Lost.* As I reread the *Second Defence* recently, I found myself wondering whether the effects that total blindness was to have upon the organ voice and the basic attitudes we feel in the three major poems had not already begun. Certainly we find them in the change from the early sonnets to those he wrote after he lost his sight.

There is little more that need detain us in the middle years. In November 1656, four and one-half years after the death of Mary Powell, Milton married Katherine Woodcock, a young woman of twenty-eight. She lived only fifteen months, dying as the result of the birth of a child who also died. In September of that year occurred the death of the Lord Protector, Oliver Cromwell. Less than two years later, the experiment of the Commonwealth ended and on May 29, 1660, Charles II was welcomed to London. During the following summer, Milton who had continued his pamphleteering in spite of his blindness, was hiding in a friend's house. Orders had been issued for his arrest, as an enemy of the state. For a time he was under arrest, but since he was not named in the Act of Indemnity—the act of oblivion, as his nephew called it—he was released and free to take up his life again, though two of his pamphlets were burned by the public hangman, as a symbol of his guilt against the monarchy. On that occasion, when Milton's work joined the long roster of "banned and burned books," we may hope that others than he remembered his own words "For books are not absolutely dead things, but do contain a potency of life in them to be as active as that soul was whose progeny they are; nay, they do preserve as in a vial the purest efficacy and extraction of that living intellect that bred them."

The Sonnets

During the twenty years between 1640, when he wrote the *Epitaphium Damonis,* and 1660, the year of King Charles' Restoration, Milton published no poetry, with the exception of the 1645 edition of his early poems. He had been thirty-one when he wrote his lament for Diodati; he was fifty-one when he went into hiding after the Restoration of His Majesty. While he may have been working on *Paradise Lost,* the only poetry that can definitely be assigned to these middle years is the small group of sonnets. Some of the early ones had been published in the *Poems* of 1645. Nearly all the others remained unpublished until 1673, the year before Milton's death, while three or four, for obvious political reasons, did not appear until 1694, long after the author's death. The most important evidence for the order in which Milton wrote them and for their dating comes from the manuscript in which Milton preserved them, the Trinity or Cambridge Manuscript, in the library of Trinity College, Cambridge.

We know that Milton had written Italian sonnets when he was very young, well before his journey to Italy. Some of these may be among the most personal of his poems if they are really to a young Italian woman with whom Milton had fallen in love, although it is equally possible that they merely represent Italian traditions Milton was following. One Italian sonnet was addressed to Diodati to whom Milton seems to confess that he, who had once scoffed, had fallen in the snare. His love, he says, is not an English girl "of golden locks, or damask cheek":

> More rare,
> The heartfelt beauties of my foreign fair,
> A mien majestic, with dark brows that show
> The tranquil lustre of a lofty mind;
> Words exquisite, of idiom more than one,
> And song.
>
> Sonnet IV (Cowper translation)

We have paused momentarily over the English sonnet, written for his birthday, when he felt that his "late spring no bud or blossom showeth." One other early English sonnet remains, Sonnet I on the nightingale, conventional and imitative enough of the Italians, which, some critics suggest, may have been intended as an introduction to the five Italian sonnets and a canzone, which combine to form a short love-sequence of a kind familiar among both Italian and English sonneteers. These early verses I shall not consider further, but, after a brief discussion of the sonnet-tradition, pass on to the sonnets we know were written early or late in the middle years.

THE SONNET TRADITION

"Scorn not the sonnet," Wordsworth warned his generation, reminding both critics and poets of their goodly heritage:

> Scorn not the Sonnet; Critic, you have frowned,
> Mindless of its just honours; with this key
> Shakespeare unlocked his heart; the melody

Of this small lute gave ease to Petrarch's wound;
A thousand times this pipe did Tasso sound;
With it Camöens soothed an exile's grief;
The Sonnet glittered a gay myrtle leaf
Amid the cypress with which Dante crowned
His visionary brow: a glow-worm lamp,
It cheered mild Spenser, call'd from Faery-land
To struggle through dark ways; and when a damp
Fell round the path of Milton, in his hand
The thing became a trumpet; whence he blew
Soul-animating strains—alas, too few!

The sonnet is one of the few forms he used for which Milton had no classical precedent or model though it is possible that Milton, like some modern critics, thought of it as a variant upon the classical epigram which it resembles in succinctness and compression. Even if we were not familiar with its history, Wordsworth's brief catalogue would tell us one reason for its inevitable appeal to Milton. It was an Italian form, the greatest practitioners of which had been Dante, Petrarch and Tasso. In England it had been adapted by many but the two English poets he mentioned would have been "authority" enough for Milton, had he needed it—"sweetest Shakespeare, Fancy's child" and "our sage and serious Spenser."

In addition to its long history in the hands of poets he admired, Milton would have been attracted to the sonnet by the limitations the form imposed upon any poet who uses it. It is one of the few English forms (Italian has many more) in which the poet's craft is taxed to the full to keep within boundaries and limitations, yet challenged to transcend those limitations by adaptation of materials to the metrical rules. The form requires the terseness Milton admired in Greek poetry, the opportunity and the challenge to say much in little. Many English poets who used the poem have suggested by analogies the restraint it implies. "What is a sonnet?" asked Richard Watson Gilder, and replied,

't is the pearly shell
That murmurs of the far-off murmuring sea;

A precious jewel carved most curiously;
It is a little picture painted well.

Dante Gabriel Rossetti also developed the traditional themes of the sonnet:

A sonnet is a coin: its face reveals
The soul,—its converse to what power 't is due:—
Whether for tribute to the august appeals
Of Life, or dower in Love's high retinue,
It serve; or, 'mid the dark wharf's cavernous breath
In Charon's palm it pay the toll to Death.

"Nuns fret not at their narrow convent room" as Wordsworth wrote in still another sonnet upon sonnets; the very limitations of the convent room symbolize the values they sought in the life they have deliberately chosen. So poets have felt for generations about the limitations imposed by the sonnet.

As Milton inherited the sonnet, he was free to choose among several forms, some Italian, some English, each having the authority of great poets. Most English students think of the Italian sonnet as being divided between an octave and a sestet, though the practice of various Italian poets seems to indicate that they were really writing two quatrains and two tercets. Since, however, there was almost universal agreement that the two quatrains must be constructed by the use of only two rhymes, we may legitimately consider the first eight lines an octave. Dante and other early and modern poets sometimes used alternate rhymes, *abab;* Petrarch did so infrequently. The octave of the Italian sonnet adopted by most English followers is *abba, abba.* The tercet offered more variety. Sometimes it too was limited to two rhymes, often arranged *cdc, cdc* or *cdc, dcd.* Not infrequently a third rhyme was added, *cde, cde; cde, dce* and other combinations were possible. Occasionally a final couplet appears, though it is far from common. The "Petrarchan sonnet," to Milton as to most of us, consists of an octave with enclosed, not alternate lines, and a sestet with three rhymes, arranged in various ways.

In England two simpler forms developed among those who did not follow the Petrarchan model. The simplest, used by Surrey and most famous in Shakespeare, consists of three quatrains, each with its own alternate rhyme, and a couplet, introducing still another rhyme: *abad, cdcd, efef, gg.* Spenser experimented with a form basically like the Surrey-Shakespeare sonnet, except that a rhyme was carried over from one quatrain to the next: *abab bcbc, cdcd, ee.* In spite of Milton's admiration for both Shakespeare and Spenser, it was natural that with his love of Italian poetry and his tendency toward the "classical" model, if there was one, he should have followed Petrarch and adapted the tighter and more difficult of the various rhyme schemes. His octave is always *abba, abba,* his sestet often limited to two rhymes, although he uses combinations of *cde* in five English sonnets. Only in one—the sonnet to Cromwell —does he use a final couplet. "On the New Forcers of Conscience," Milton's one "tailed sonnet," concludes with a triple rhyme in the first coda, a couplet in the second.

As the sonnet grew in Milton's "right hand"—a poetic release from the "left-hand" prose—it became a form characteristically Miltonic, not only in its becoming a "trumpet," as Wordsworth said, but in its rhythmic dexterity and virtuosity. As we have seen in *Lycidas,* the paragraph rather than the sentence seems to have been Milton's unit and we find ourselves thinking of his best sonnets as beautifully articulated paragraphs rather than as a series of couplets, quatrains, tercets. Unlike various earlier and later poets, Milton did not feel a necessary separation between octave and sestet. More and more, he tends to enjambment—carrying over the sense from either the eighth or the ninth line. In some of his finest sonnets, for example the two on his blindness, the one on Cromwell and the sonnet on the massacre of the Piedmontese, we notice that a new sentence, introducing the theme of the sestet, begins in the middle of either the eighth or ninth line, sometimes implying a dramatic change in mood.

In considering Milton's sonnets, I shall divide them into three groups, which I call conventional, personal, and political, although there is some inevitable overlapping between the first two. Sonnet XVII to Sir Henry Vane is really a conventional sonnet of tribute, but because of the political references I shall put it into the third group. In the numbering of the sonnets I follow, as do most modern editors, the numbering of John S. Smart, which is based, so far as possible, upon the order in which they were preserved in Milton's manuscript.

CONVENTIONAL SONNETS

The conventional sonnets follow time-honored traditions though in Milton's case the themes are not those most frequent in Italian and English sonnets—love. They are largely tributes to a particular man or woman, except for Sonnet XX which is in the classical tradition of "inviting a friend to supper."

Sonnet IX, "Lady that in the Prime"

"Lady that in the prime," has been called in some editions "To a Virtuous Young Lady." Since this was one of the sonnets included in the *Poems* of 1645, we can date it merely as being earlier than that year. The subject has not been identified, though various suggestions have been made. In spite of the generic word, "Lady," this sonnet is addressed to a young girl, probably the daughter of a family friend who may have confided to Milton that the girl had been criticized by her young friends for what seemed to them priggishness (lines 6-7). Particularly if she was just entering her teens, she may have seemed to other youngsters a creature much too bright and good for human nature's daily food. In his words of comfort and encouragement, Milton uses more Biblical allusions than in any other sonnet—Biblical allusions were hardly sonnet conventions. He reminds her of other virtuous young women, recalling the story of Ruth and Naomi in the Old Testament (Ruth I. 14), of Mary, the sister of Martha (Luke X. 42) who chose the better part. The sestet develops the parable of the wise and foolish virgins (Matthew XXV. 1-13), the foolish who wasted the oil for their lamps, the wise who saved it. Even the opening quatrain suggests the Bible, since Milton combines an old classical *topos* of "Hill Difficulty" with various Christian analogues, particularly Matthew VII. 13-14: "Strait is the gate and narrow is the way that leadeth unto life, and few there be that find it." (Notice the rhyme of "Ruth . . . ruth" in lines 5 and 8, one of the very rare examples of identical rhyme in Milton.)

Sonnet X, To the Lady Margaret Ley

This was also published in the *Poems* of 1645. The sonnet is a tribute to a lady, but even more to her illustrious father. Both are readily identified. Lady Margaret Ley and her husband, Captain John Hobson, were Milton's neighbors when the two families lived in Aldersgate Street. Edward Phillips said, "This lady, being a woman of great wit and ingenuity, had a particular honour for him, and took much delight in his company, as likewise Captain Hobson, her husband, a very accomplished gentleman." Lady Margaret, as the sonnet says, was "daughter to that good Earl," the Earl of Marlborough, who had had a distinguished career as lawyer, judge, statesman. As Lord Chief Justice, he had presided over the bribery trial of Francis Bacon, Lord Chancellor, in 1622 and pronounced sentence. Under Charles I he held the offices of Lord High Treasurer and Lord President of the Council, retiring

from the latter in 1628, shortly before his death. As Milton's sonnet suggests, his last days were bitterly unhappy because of the
"sad breaking of that Parliament,"—the forcible dissolution of the
Parliament in 1629—which marked the sharp break between
Charles and the Parliamentary leaders, and was really the beginning of the end, so far as monarchy and arbitrary government
were concerned. There is no other evidence than Milton's words
that the political crisis hastened Marlborough's death, although
Lady Margaret may have told Milton so. In the tribute to Marlborough (line 3) that he lived "unstained with gold or fee," we may
perhaps find a covert allusion to the Bacon trial. In lines 6-8 Milton's allusive mind goes back to Greek history for an analogue to
Marlborough's death. When Philip of Macedon defeated Thebes
and Athens in the Battle of Chaeronea in 338 B.C., Milton implies
that it was a "dishonest," that is, a "shameful," victory since it
marked the end of freedom in the Greek city states. He compares
Marlborough's death (l. 8) with that of the great Greek orator,
Isocrates, who was reported to have starved himself to death after
what he felt was the disaster of Chaeronea. The sonnet ends with a
tribute to the daughter in whom the moral virtues of the father are
"living yet."

Sonnet XIII. Mr. Henry Lawes

This sonnet, written in 1646, was, with the exception of those
early enough for the *Poems* of 1645, the only poem published
during Milton's middle years. It appeared, with other tributes, in
the volume of Lawes' *Choice Psalms* in 1648. Milton's admiration
for Lawes, which we remember from the *Comus* period, had not
diminished because Lawes remained an ardent Royalist. His
brother William, also a musician, had been killed in the battle at
Chester. Milton rightly praises Lawes' setting of lyrics to music. Unlike some composers of that period and much later, he adapted the

music to the words, rather than forcing the accent of the words to music (a process that many of us often notice in familiar hymns). Lawes, says Milton, scanned as a poet should scan, not as Midas might have done. (According to Ovid, Midas' ears were transformed to those of an ass because he preferred the piping of Pan to the music of Apollo.) Lawes was never guilty of "committing" —that is, setting in conflict—short and long stresses. On the manuscript Milton wrote "misjoining" as a possible alternative to "committing." The allusion to a "story" (1. 11) might have remained unknown had not this line been annotated by Milton himself in the only marginal note he ever appended to a poem. In the edition of the *Choice Psalms* Milton explained: "The story of Ariadne set by him in music," calling attention to the fact that Lawes had set to music William Cartwright's *The Complaint of Ariadne*. In the last three lines of the sonnet, Milton's memory goes back to a scene in the *Purgatorio* (II.76-117) in which Dante met the spirit of Casella, a Florentine musician, who had set some of Dante's canzoni to music. Milton implies that his friend Lawes would deserve an even higher place on the progress to Paradise.

Sonnet XIV. Mrs. Catharine Thomason

Many students of literature and history who have never heard of Mrs. Catharine Thomason will recognize the last name because her husband, George Thomason collected the "Thomason Tracts," more than 22,000 pamphlets published between 1642 and 1661, now deposited in the British Museum. Thomason's original collection included *Areopagitica* and various others of Milton's tracts, all of them gifts of the author. The fact that this sonnet, like the one to the virtuous young lady, is phrased in basically Christian terms led John Smart to suggest that the girl may have been Mrs. Thomason's daughter, in which case she would have been a child not older than twelve when the sonnet was addressed to her.

Sonnet XX. Lawrence of Virtuous Father . . .

Edward Phillips noted in his memoir of his uncle that one friend who often visited Milton was "young Lawrence, the son of him that was President of Oliver's Council, to whom there is a sonnet among the rest in his printed poems." Henry Lawrence, the "virtuous father," had two sons, Edward and Henry. Earlier biographers were inclined to think that the subject of the sonnet was Henry, who outlived his father, but evidence presented by John Smart makes it much more probable that the young man, who often came to Milton's house, was the older son Edward, far more serious and intellectual than his brother. This remarkable young man was elected to Parliament in 1656—the year of Milton's sonnet—when he was only twenty-three. Unfortunately he died the following year at the age of twenty-four. In theme and detail, this sonnet follows closely the form of "invitation to a friend," particularly the pattern established by Horace in *Epistles* I. ix. The form was a popular one among English poets. The student may compare Milton's use of the convention with Ben Jonson's "Inviting a Friend to Supper." Whether because of the sonnet's limitation of length or because of Milton's more ascetic way of life, we find no such table as Jonson's, loaded with "olives, capers or some better salad" serving as *hors d'oeuvres* to meats in profusion; mutton, perhaps a hare, fowl of various sorts from "a short-legged hen" through larks to partridge, pheasant, or woodcock, not to mention "digestive cheese" which the gargantuan guest must have needed by the time he reached it in his menu. At both Milton's and Jonson's tables wine was served but obviously in greater quantity and variety at Jonson's than at Milton's. Jonson's guest would have heard Virgil, Tacitus or Livy read aloud. Milton's friend Lawrence listened to, perhaps joined in, music. It is interesting, even in this classically conventional sonnet, to catch the Biblical strain in "the lily and rose, that neither sowed nor spun." Like Jonson and many others in the tradition, Milton ends with a bit of mild moralizing, the "lesson" of which depends upon the meaning of "spare" (l. 13) which Milton uses in a sense now lost in English. Smart would make Milton more austere than he probably was by interpreting it, "forbear." More recent commentators interpret it as "afford." Mild moralizing indeed in the Horation vein; but similar enough to what we shall find in the next sonnet, written to a young man who had been one of Milton's students, to make us wonder whether Lawrence, the "virtuous son," had once also been a pupil of Milton's.

Sonnet XXI. "Cyriack, whose Grandsire . . ."

This is one of two sonnets addressed to the same person, the other of which will be considered among the "Personal Sonnets." It bears a slight resemblance to the sonnet to Lady Margaret Ley in that a parent or grandparent is also praised. Otherwise the Horatian vein more closely resembles the sonnet to Lawrence we have just read in that the poet is writing to a much younger friend, this time one we know to have been *in statu pupillari*. The "grandsire" was Sir Edward Coke, Chief Justice of the King's Bench one of the great jurists of England, and (another passing reminiscence to the Ley sonnet) the arch enemy of Sir Francis Bacon, in whose political downfall he was undoubtedly involved. Cyriack Skinner had been one of the first pupils in Milton's school, and affection between teacher and pupil continued as long as Milton lived. We know that he served Milton as amanuensis, and William Riley Parker believes that he was the author of the "anonymous" life of Milton, which Miss Helen Darbishire attributed to Milton's other nephew, John Phillips. In the light moralizing of this, as in the previous sonnet, we catch the tone of a friendly schoolmaster delivering a little lecture to the young, and if we interpret the "spare" of the preceding sonnet as "afford," we find the "lesson" much the same.

The line, "Let Euclid rest and Archimedes pause," may be a laughing reference to the interest Skinner had showed in mathematics when he was at Milton's school, and the next line, "And what the Swede intend, and what the French," to Skinner's mature interest in international affairs. In spite of the fact that in 1655, the date of this sonnet, Sweden was campaigning against the Poles and many things were happening in France under Cardinal Mazarin, the lines probably were not intended to refer to anything specific. Milton is following the Horatian pattern of admonition to the young, particularly *Ode*s II. xi, in which Horace bids Quintus Hirpinus forget the warlike Cantabrians and the Scythians and remember that he is young and youth is fleeting. Any student educated in Milton's school would have caught the echo.

PERSONAL SONNETS

Again my division is arbitrary since, of course, some of the political sonnets are personal, dealing as they do with Milton's own works or with his highly personal opinions. I group them as I do in part because the political sonnets lead us into problems of political or religious history so that they can best be treated together, and in part because these "personal" sonnets are a small group of *private* reflections on Milton's part concerning either his blindness or his dead wife.

Three sonnets, the Prologues in *Paradise Lost*, some choruses and speeches in *Samson Agonistes*, and the long passage in the *Second Defence*, already discussed, give us our chief knowledge of Milton's blindness and his attitudes toward it. Recent editors date both sonnets on his blindness 1655, but I am of the group who still feel that the first sonnet may have been written around 1652, in spite of its place in the manuscript and other evidence that has been offered for 1655. The mood reflected in this most familiar of his sonnets must have been one he often experienced when he was facing the calamity for the first time. He must have believed, indeed, that the great work for which he had been "called" would never be written.

Sonnet XIX. "When I Consider . . ."

In structure, this is one of the three most masterly of Milton's sonnets, reminding us of the architectonic expertness of *Lycidas*. I have said that Milton's basic principle in structure is the paragraph rather than the sentence, but in this case I find a remarkable example of a sentence that is a verse-paragraph or a verse-paragraph that is a sentence. I hope that the reader will forgive a personal digression, because I think that my youthful pleasure in my "discovery" of the structure of this sonnet may be shared by others. When I was still in grammar school, we were required to analyze and parse in the old-fashioned way, a fashion long outmoded but to my mind, like many other "antiques," extremely valuable. On "exhibition days," when parents and friends came to visit, each of us was told off to perform some task in public, and since I—who could not sew or draw or do anything really useful—*could* analyze and parse, I was told that I might quietly diagram on the blackboard the longest sentence I could find. Among the many books on my father's shelves, over which I pored for days, was this sonnet, fortunately for my theory in an old-fashioned text. If you will make a simple substitution, you will read the sonnet as I first read it: instead of periods, use semicolons, and reduce the capital letters to lower case. Then you will find that the sonnet really is what my old-fashioned editor and I thought it was—one magnificent compound-complex sentence. It took me the whole afternoon and the largest blackboard in the classroom to prove it but prove it I did to my complete satisfaction as I excitedly but carefully drew one of those intricate trees we used to create in diagramming, with the vertical line indicating subject, predicate and object, and all those fascinating angle lines growing as the modifiers grew—a tree as intricate as Ygdrasil (of which I had never then heard), the tree whose roots and branches bind together heaven, earth and hell. In my compound-complex diagram the basic structure on the vertical line is: "I ask; Patience replies." All the rest will fall into place, sprung from one father and mother, these two simple phrases. Enough of personal digression except to say that this was my very youthful introduction to the art and craft of a great poet, which has increased over all these years.

The metaphor around which the sonnet is developed is the parable of the talents in Matthew XXV. 14-30, in which the unprofitable servant, who buried in the earth the money his master had given him, was cast out into darkness. "That one talent which is death to hide," implies, of course, the double meaning of a *talent* as a piece of money and the other connotation of *talent* as the gift of genius, which Milton believed God had given him. As Smart points out (*Milton's Sonnets,* p. 108) the parable of the talents was in Milton's mind when he wrote that early sonnet on his birthday, since a letter of Milton's to a friend, with which he enclosed it, referred to "the terrible seizing of him that hid the talent" with Christ's command that all men should labor while it is light. That early sonnet ended on a note of resignation to the will of God:

> All is, if I have grace to use it so
> As ever in my great Task-Master's eye.

The sonnet on his blindness proceeds from grief through questioning to final resignation, but both mood and meaning are far more profound than they had been in the youthful reflections on his birthday. Milton had labored with all his might while it was still light, but darkness of a different sort had fallen before the working-day was over—before half his working-days should have been over. Was the laborer still responsible for increasing the talent which he could no longer see? We must remember that blindness was a far greater impediment to Milton than it might have been to a poet of another "school" to whom poetry might literally have been the spontaneous overflow of powerful feeling. Milton was not only a "classical" poet; he believed that one who would write a poem "doctrinal to a nation" must be a "learned" poet. For his great poem he needed to turn to books, as does a scholar, who is far more dependent on his eyes than is a novelist or lyric poet. When total darkness descended, he must have believed there was no possibility of his continuing with the great work he had laid aside at the call of his party. For a time he could only submit, saying with Job, "The Lord gave and the Lord hath taken away. Blessed be the name of the Lord." In the reply of Patience in the sonnet, Milton expresses his resignation to God's will in terms of the hierarchy of angels we shall find in *Paradise Lost*. Some angels

> in God's presence, nearest to His throne,
> Stand ready at command, and are His eyes
> That run through all the Heavens or down to the Earth
> Bear His swift errands over moist and dry,
> O'er sea and land.

(P.L. III. 649-653)

But in the Heaven of *Paradise Lost,* as we shall see, are other angels, sometimes, but not always, Seraphim and Cherubim, who are angels not of action but of contemplation. As among angels, so among men who serve God on earth, there must be those who, no longer able to be God's "eyes," serve in some other way: "They also serve who only stand and wait." Here, as so often, we find a double meaning, for in addition to the connotation that we read into the word, Milton is remembering the meaning of "wait on" as used so often in the Bible: "Wait on the Lord; be of good courage and He shall strengthen thy heart. . . . Wait, I say, on the Lord." (Psalm XXVII. 14.)

Sonnet XXII. To Cyriack Skinner

The second sonnet on his blindness was apparently written on the anniversary of the day on which Milton had been forced to realize that his blindness was total, three years earlier. Addressed to his former student, the lines are in a very different vein from the other sonnet inscribed to Skinner in the same year. Here, as in the passage in *Paradise Lost* on the "drop serene," Milton tells us that, whatever the cause of his blindness, his eyes remained clear to outward view. As we shall see in some of the Prologues to *Paradise Lost* and some lines in *Samson Agonistes,* he laments first the loss of light—of sun or moon or star—and then, as in his sonnet to his wife, his inability to see the faces of men and women around him. The mood of this sonnet is quite different from that of the preceding one. This is not quiet, almost passive, resignation to the will of God. This is the "true warfaring Christian" who will fight on, the mood in which he had imperiously replied in the preceding year in the *Second Defence* to enemies who had taunted him that his blindness was the judgment of God upon him:

> I considered that many had purchased a less good by a greater evil . . . that though I am blind, I might still discharge the most honorable duties, the performance of which, as it is something more durable than glory, ought to be an object of superior admiration and esteem. . . . I have been enabled to do the will of God.
>
> (p. 180)

"What supports me?" He answers, not as Patience had once replied to him, but proudly, in full consciousness of his service to his people and to God in the deliberate sacrifice of his eyes:

> The conscience, friend, to have lost them overplied
> In Liberty's defence, my noble task,
> Of which all Europe talks from side to side.

Milton was not exaggerating. He had humbled and abased the great Salmasius, toppling the intellectual giant of Europe from his proud place, and his fame in Europe was even greater than in his own country.

Milton's is not a personal and vainglorious boasting. He is exulting that it was he who had been chosen for a great mission, and that he had performed it to his fullest ability. The most striking difference between the two sonnets lies right here: the first in language and mood echoes the New Testament; the second is the temper of many passages in the Old Testament. It is the mood in which he wrote the first *Defence*, when he was speaking as David had spoken to the Philistine Goliath, enemy of his people and of his God: "Thou comest to me with a sword and with a spear, and with a javelin; but I come to thee in the name of Jehovah of hosts, the God of the armies of Israel, whom thou hast defied. This day will Jehovah deliver thee into my hand. . . . that all the earth may know that there is a God in Israel."

Here is the sense of triumph and exultation of one who has fought the good fight, who has kept the faith. If he has not finished the whole course, he has not given his eyes in vain. If he has not been called to be a great poet, he has been called to avenge the adversaries of his party, who in his mind were the antagonists of God. In the two sonnets on his blindness we feel the same difference Professor Tillyard feels between the two *Defences*, and our minds, like his, go forward to *Samson Agonistes*, in which both moods appear. For a time Samson, like Job, suffers despondency and discouragement, from which he rises to a period of submission and patience, first passive, then active. As his strength returns, so does his courage and a rising optimism he cannot fully explain:

> Be of good courage, I begin to feel
> Some rousing motions in me which dispose
> To something extraordinary my thoughts.

> (*S.A.* 1381-83)

The sestet of the sonnet marks a rising line in Milton, as in Job's, "Though He slay me, yet will I trust in Him." Milton had fulfilled one calling; perhaps he was still to fulfill the other.

Sonnet XXIII. Methought I saw . . .

I have said that Milton's conventional sonnets did not follow the convention most common among sonneteers—that of love—and that he wrote no love-sonnets in English. Yet in a different way, this is a love-sonnet, the tenderest, the most private of all his personal sonnets, and the most poignant of the sonnets on his blindness. Before considering its structure and mood, it is necessary to enter into the controversy I have mentioned, which was caused by William Riley Parker's suggestion that the subject was not, as we had always supposed, Milton's second wife, Katherine Woodcock whom he married after he was blind, but Mary Powell. Professor Parker will forgive me, I hope, if I over-simplify his argument for our present purposes. His contention is based chiefly upon the lines:

Mine, as whom washed from spot of child-bed taint,
Purification in the Old Law did save.

Milton's reference here is to Leviticus XII, 2-5, in which were laid down laws concerning women after childbirth, some of which were carried over into Christianity in what is called "The Churching of Women." According to Professor Parker, the phrase, "washed from child-bed taint" could apply only to Mary Powell who died three days after her child was born, and not to Katherine Woodcock, who lived three months after the birth of her child. Professor Parker, and others who follow him, quite naturally read lines 7-8

And such as *yet once more* I trust to have
Full sight of her in Heaven without restraint,

as implying that Milton is referring to a wife he had seen, not to one he married after he became blind.

Mary Powell, we remember, had returned to her husband in the summer of 1645. She died in May, 1652, three months after Milton's blindness was total. During these years she had borne three daughters who survived her, a son who had died at the age of two, and the child who had died with her. Milton remained a widower for four and a half years before marrying Katherine Woodcock, who lived only a year and a half, dying in February 1658. The sonnet to his dead wife was written in that year, though we do not know the month. (Her daughter, christened October 19, 1657, was buried March 20, 1658.) It is difficult to imagine Milton or any other man writing his most personal and moving sonnet to a first wife a few weeks or months after the death of the second. If, as Parker and others suggest, the reconciliation with Mary Powell had been such that Milton deeply treasured her memory, it seems more likely that he would have written the sonnet shortly after her death when he was suffering the first shock of blindness. The theory of happy reconciliation between husband and wife is hardly borne out by the legal documents filed after Milton's death in connection with his will, in which he left his estate to his third and surviving wife, after these words, as reported by his lawyer-brother Christopher:

> The portion due to me from Mr. Powell, my former wife's father, I leave to the unkind children I had by her, having received no part of it: but my meaning is, they shall have no other benefit of my estate than the said portion, and what I have besides done for them; they having been very undutiful to me.

Two final points may be made in connection with the "washed from spot of child-bed taint." Whatever the Church or the doctors may have found concerning Katherine's death, Edward Phillips considered that both women had died from the same cause. He said, "In this House his first Wife dying in Childbed, he Married a

Second, who after a Year's time died in Childbed also." Phillps was undoubtedly speaking as any layman of his age would have spoken, using the same phrase for the wife who had died almost immediately after bearing a child, and the one whose death was unquestionably a remote result of childbirth. The Puritan Milton, with his attitude toward various sacraments of the Roman or Established Church, would hardly have been seriously concerned whether one wife or the other had been "churched," but since the reference in the sonnet is to the Old Law, we should remember that Leviticus laid down a period of thirty-three days of purification after the birth of a son, sixty-six after the birth of a daughter. Katherine Woodcock had lived beyond sixty-six days, and may even have been "churched."

At the opposite extreme to Parker is Leo Spitzer (*Hopkins Review,* IV [1951] 20-22), who thinks that the sonnet is not about any real woman. Milton was merely following conventions of Dante's and Petrarch's use of the *donna angelica,* the ideal of a poet in a heavenly vision. But enough of controversy. I shall continue, with others, to read the sonnet, as I believe it was written, as a tribute to Katherine Woodcock shortly after her death. The basic figure of the first four and last six lines is drawn from the legend of Alcestis, particularly as the story was treated in Euripides' play of that name. Alcestis, wife of Admetus, had given her life in place of her husband's. Hercules fought for her and brought her back, stipulating that Admetus agree to marry this apparently strange woman without putting back her veil until after the ceremony. In Milton's poem the "late espoused saint" appeared to him veiled. Blind students whom I have been privileged to teach have told me that it is a frequent experience for those who have lost their sight in adulthood to dream of people they have never seen with faces veiled or clouded in one way or another. Mr. Parker and others of his school read the "late" of "late espoused saint" in the general sense in which we use it of speaking of the dead: "My late wife," for example. But "late" was frequently used as an adverb, so that "late espoused" can equally well mean "the wife I had lately married." Milton had never seen Katherine Woodcock in reality, but he had apparently recently seen her in a dream, in which her face was clouded. He trusts that he will have "full sight of her in Heaven" "once more" when the mists have been cleared from his eyes. Admetus had been more fortunate than Milton; his wife though "pale and faint," had been saved from death, but Katherine Woodcock, "pale and faint" had slipped away, not to return in this life. Both husbands saw their wives with veiled faces, but when Milton in his dream eagerly put out his hand to remove the veil, he experienced the tragedy felt each morning by the recently blind. In the Prologue to Book III of *Paradise Lost,* after suggesting that during the night he had been with the Muse, he seems to recall much the same situation as in the sonnet:

> but not to me returns
> Day, or the sweet approach of even or morn,
> Or sight of vernal bloom or summer's rose
> Or flocks or herds *or human face divine.*

In the sonnet he suggests that this was the first time he had dreamed of his dead wife. Like Admetus, he would gladly have put forth his hand to see the "love, sweetness, goodness" he had felt during their short married life. At that eager moment he woke to the daily tragic realization of the blind, expressed in the poignant last lines:

> But oh as to embrace me she inclined,
> I waked, she fled, and day brought back my night.

In the masterly interweaving of classical and Christian themes and material, the last sonnet takes us back to *Lycidas,* in which pagan and Christian are inextricably intertwined. Basically the dominant figure is classical legend. The lines on the Old Law take us back to the Bible. Milton's "saint" is in a Christian heaven, but while her costume recalls Alcestis, it does so with overtones of the vision of Revelation VII. 13-14:

Those that are arrayed in the white robes, who are they, and whence come they? . . . These are they that come out of great tribulation and they washed their robes and made them white in the blood of the lamb.

POLITICAL SONNETS

Sonnet VIII. "Captain or Colonel, or Knight in Arms"

Nothing can better remind us of Milton's cloistered youth than the tone of this sonnet against its background. We remember that Milton said that he had changed his plans for further travel when the "melancholy intelligence" reached him of growing unrest in England. But for a time he remained as aloof from the practical problems of the state as he had always been. True, the year before the sonnet was written he had entered the war of words with his anti-episcopal tracts. But on August 22, 1643 Civil War became an actuality. According to the manuscript Milton originally considered as a title, "On his door when the city expected an attack," replaced by "When the assault was intended to the city," neither of which was used when the sonnet was published in the *Poems* of 1645. It is true that there was little chance for success on the part of Charles' forces. "When the assault was intended to the city," they found themselves facing a hastily assembled but well drilled militia of over 20,000. Neither side attacked, and in a short time the King withdrew. Nevertheless, although there proved no real danger, there was natural alarm and suspense in London. I suspect that the tone of the sonnet was less a result of Milton's "inflexible composure," to which Smart pays tribute, (*Milton's Sonnets*, p. 57) than the fact that he was still spiritually dwelling in his impregnable ivory tower with *Il Penseroso.*

Scansion of the first line shows that Milton, like many others, pronounced "Colonel" in three syllables. Derived through French, this spelling was used alternatively with "Coronel," from which we have our modern pronunciation. Milton is saying: If the commanding officer, whoever he may be, will spare this house of a poet, he will be rewarded, since the poet has power through his art to perpetuate the memory of his benefactor. When his city was in peril, "the education of a poet" sent Milton's memory back to classical analogues. At the time of the sack of Thebes in 336 B.C., the "great Emathian conqueror," Alexander the Great,—so legend if not history tells—spared only one house, that of the poet Pindar. And, according to Plutarch, when Athens was captured by the Spartans in 404 B.C., the conquerors were about to raze the city and turn the district into a sheep-pasture until "a man of Phocis" began to sing the first chorus in Euripides' *Electra:*

> Electra, Agammemnon's child, I come
> Unto thy desert home.

At which, according to Plutarch, "they were all melted with compassion," remembering the glorious past of the city.

It is fitting that the sonnet should first have appeared in the *Poems* of 1645 that hark back to Milton's cloistered youth. One can hardly imagine Milton, the statesman, whose life became so inextricably involved with that of his country, publishing it for the first time in 1673.

Sonnet XI. "A Book was writ . . ."

We are already familiar with the situation that provoked this sonnet and the next one—Milton's publication of the *Divorce Tracts,* one of which he called *Tetrachordon.* The word, a technical musical term, meant a combination of four notes into a chord. In the tract Milton had analyzed the four chief passages in Scripture, which were interpreted by Roman Catholics and Anglicans as interdicting divorce, in such as a way as to prove to his own satisfaction that they did no such thing. To Milton, with his knowledge of Greek and music, the word was a familiar one; but many of his contemporaries had found it as unintelligible as it seems to most modern readers. As you read the sonnet, notice that its irony is deliberately enhanced by some of the rhymes. Inveighing against what seemed to him illiterates, Milton cuts his pattern to fit their shoddy cloth, and with the word "Tetrachordon" rhymes "pored on," "word on," "Gordon." In addition he makes rhymes for "style," not only by using the internal rhyme, "while," but by deliberately dividing between two lines "Mile-End Green," a familiar word to any Londoner. These are tricks of Samuel Butler, of W. S. Gilbert, in our time of Ogden Nash.

The setting of the sonnet is among bookstalls where passers-by did much of their casual browsing, if not their buying. It is an impatient rejoinder on Milton's part to some of the bewildered readers he may actually have seen puzzling over the title without bothering to read the book. In his tracts Milton had been dealing with a fairly new and certainly provocative subject—justification of divorce. He had gone to pains over both form and style; the tract was as compact as he could make it, "woven close." Clearly, it had not proved a "best seller." For a time it had found a small audience among intellects that could appreciate it, but now, as if it had been "remaindered"—as we might say—it is tossed on the rubbish heap of a stall, where an ignoramus may turn it over, getting no farther than the title: "Bless us! what a word on A title-page is this." He is followed by other stupid oafs who have no intention of buying, but "spelling false"—misread it, and, stupid as they are, take almost as much time spelling out the title as it would require a walk to Mile-End Green, the outward limit of London. Into the faces of those to whom "Tetrachordon" seemed a hard word, Milton throws a group of Scottish proper names of a kind that were

G

more and more infiltrating into London from the barbarous North. Some were names of real people, though "Galasp" is unknown as a proper name. Possibly it was a mutilated form of "Gillespie," though I rather suspect it was merely a satiric invention of Milton's as another rhyme for "asp" and "grasp." Imagine, says Milton, how these Scottish names would have sounded to Quintilian, great orator and authority upon usage, who had particularly warned against the use of proper names of foreign origin, "uncouth" in both the seventeenth-century and the modern usage. Milton is saying in effect what Matthew Arnold said in *The Function of Criticism* about "the growth of such hideous names as Higginbottom, Stiggins, Bugg . . . by the Ilissus there was no Wragg, poor thing!" Byron put it more succinctly: "Oh, Amos Cottle—Phoebus, what a name!"

Milton's little peroration is addressed to the soul of Sir John Cheek, the great English humanist of the preceding century, first Professor of Greek at Cambridge, and tutor to King Edward VI. The compression of the penultimate lines is puzzling enough that such authorities as John Smart and J. H. Hanford interpret the last three lines in opposite ways. Mr. Hanford reads: "Thy age did not, as ours does, hate learning." Mr. Smart quotes at some length to emphasize the fact that "the introduction of the New Learning into England was accompanied by much prejudice and hostility," and mentions a statement of Cheek's, "The Greek language was hateful to many, and is so now. . . . The good men of the present age abhor the scholarly mind." Smart's reading of the line is: *"They hated not learning worse than toad or asp*—but as much as they hated either." Two of my ingenious students have suggested a slight change in typesetting, one of which will bear out Hanford's, the other, Smart's reading. For Hanford, let the printer set: "Hated not-learning worse than toad or asp"; for Smart, "Hated not learning—worse than toad or asp." Milton, writing in ironic mood as he was, might well have approved one or the other.

Sonnet XII. On the Same

The previous sonnet dealt specifically with one tract. In this one, Milton is thinking of the series as a whole. More deeply serious than the first one, the mood of which is irony and irritation, it has yet some of the same quality of invective against a generation of barbarians, which we feel particularly in the cacophonous medley of animal-noises in line 4, and in the deliberate use of such words as "hogs" and "bawl." We know that Milton had every reason to be both startled and deeply disturbed by the reception of his tracts among members of his own party. Milton was not only mentioned by name in the order of Parliament for licensing the press, but he was held up to public censure by Herbert Palmer, a spokesman for the Puritan party, in a sermon preached to both Houses of Parliament. The State was urged to allow no toleration of the new theory of divorce, "of which a wicked book is abroad and uncensured, though deserving to be burnt." Already disillusioned by the attitude of the Presbyterians, Milton shows himself in this sonnet and the next turning further and further from the right wing of the Puritan party. The theme of his *Divorce Tracts,* as well as *Areopagitica* and *Of Education,* he had said, was *liberty*. What he had hoped for his country was the liberty for which he once believed his party was ready to fight and die. Instead of the applause he had expected for his frank statement of opinion, he heard a hiss of ugly sounds, "Of owls and cuckoos, asses, apes, and dogs," all with ugly voices, and each one traditionally a symbol: the owl of ignorance, the cuckoo of ingratitude and vanity, the ass, of stupidity and obstinacy, the ape of empty mockery, and the dog of quarrelsomeness. To carry out the animal imagery, Milton goes back to classical legend and recalls a story of Ovid, that Jove, father of Diana (moon goddess) and Apollo (sun god) turned into frogs a group of peasants who refused to help them and their mother,

Latona. Such was the thanks of his party. This, Milton reflects, is what one gets for casting pearls before swine. They have bawled for freedom, but they have no idea what freedom really implies. In the lines that follow Milton makes one of his famous distinctions, echoing, as so often when he speaks of liberty, the words of Christ in the Gospel according to John: "Ye shall know the truth, and the truth shall make you free." The freedom they wish is not freedom but the abuse of it, the licence for every man to do exactly what he wants to do. True liberty is a hard thing, to be attained only by those who are wise and good.

"On the New Forcers of Conscience under the Long Parliament"

This sonnet bears no number, probably because it is the one sonnet written by Milton which is not in the conventional form of fourteen lines. In many modern editions it is printed after Sonnet XII, the place it holds in the Trinity Manuscript. The form is that of the *Sonetto Caudato,* a sonnet with a coda or tail. Practitioners of the form did not limit themselves to one tail; Milton has two (lines 15-17, 18-20). He might have added others if he had wished to do so. Among the Italians it was largely a humorous form, or as in Milton, satiric. Continuing the theme of *liberty* in the preceding sonnet, Milton is here particularly attacking the Presbyterians in the Westminister Assembly, from whom he is departing further and further.

In 1643, the Long Parliament, after abolishing episcopacy—the government of the Church by Archbishops and Bishops—proposed to establish another form which Milton satirizes as "a Classic Hierarchy" (*Presbytery* and *Classis* could be used interchangeably), in which the governors would be a group of Presbyters, or elders. Sharp opposition arose from a group of Independents (with whom

Milton was in accord at this time) not only on the form of Church-government but even more on the question whether Independent congregations would be permitted to exist outside the national Church, and to what extent freedom of belief would be tolerated. The Presbyterians refused freedom of dissent and demanded conformity to the Established Church, while the Independents continued to fight for freedom of conscience.

As in *Areopagitica,* so in his tailed sonnet, Milton stresses the irony of the fact that Presbyterians who had battled to throw off the yoke of episcopacy were now coming to practice the very abuses against which they had fought. For example, "**Plurality**" (or "Pluralism," the practice of holding two or more benefices at once) had been one of the Anglican abuses against which Presbyterians had rebelled. Now they are doing it themselves, says Milton, and it becomes clear that they really did not detest the practice but rather "envied" this easy way of increasing their incomes. In the lines that follow, Milton states the position of the Independents against the Presbyterians who sought to confine all men within the straitjackets of conformity and refused to permit the liberty of conscience demanded by the Independents. They would force our consciences that Christ set free; again our ears catch the echo of the Gospel according to John.

In the lines introducing proper names (8-12) Milton attacks a group of the most reactionary Presbyterians: Adam Stuart, a Scot, one of whose pamphlets was signed only with his initials ("mere A.S."); Samuel Rutherford, Professor of Divinity at St. Andrews, whose pamphlets threatened drastic persecution of nonconformists; (a later anti-toleration tract was directed chiefly against Roger Williams and Jeremy Taylor); Thomas Edwards ("shallow Edwards"), Puritan preacher and pamphleteer; and "Scotch What-d'ye-call," Robert Baillie, another Scottish tractarian. During the recent skirmish, these had been the most vocal and most rigid of the Presbyterian foes of toleration. Against these he opposes, by implication, a group of his own more liberal Independents,

Men whose life, learning, faith, and pure intent
Would have been held in high esteem with Paul.

He is referring in particular to a group of Independent clergymen
(William Bridge, Jeremiah Burroughs, Thomas Goodwin, Philip
Nye, Sidrach Simpson) who had recently published a joint mani-
festo, the *Apologetical Narration,* sharply opposing the regulations
proposed by the Presbyterians and demanding toleration and freedom of conscience.

The *Sonetto Caudato* concludes with a sharp warning to the
Presbyterians. The Independents will discover all the tricks and
plots of these men. The Parliament may stop short of ("baulk")
cutting off their ears, as William Prynne's had been cut off, but
(here Milton goes back first to the Old Testament, then to the
New) the sharp shears of Parliament will "clip your phylacteries."
These had originally been small boxes containing passages from
Mosaic Law, worn on forehead and arm by pious Jews, but to Christians they had become, as Jesus Christ implied (Matthew XXIII.
5) symbols of hypocrisy among men who pretended to be spiritual
leaders but who actually, according to Jesus, "love the chief places
of feasts, and the chief seats in the synagogue." As in *Lycidas,*
Milton is accusing the corrupt clergy of creeping, intruding and
climbing into the fold "for their bellies' sake." He succeeded magnificently in *Lycidas* but failed here. With the exception of the last
coda, this is far inferior to most of his other sonnets. However it
may have impressed contemporaries who would have understood
at first hearing the many covert allusions and double meanings, it
is too "occasional" to live long after the period of controversy that
provoked it. In this way it is like those tractates of Milton's which
are now read only by the historians, not like the great prose of the
Second Defence and the *Areopagitica* which transcend the alterca-
tion of an age and remain "doctrinal to a nation." Embroiled in
controversy Milton slaps back at his adversaries with name-calling,
vituperation, personal invective, never rising to the heights of
which he is elsewhere so capable, like the great prophets of doom.

Only in the last line do we momentarily feel the power of words of which he was usually master:

When they shall read this clearly in your charge:
New Presbyter is but old Priest writ large.

The "tailed sonnet," like the scorpion, carries its sting in its tail. Even a schoolboy in Milton's day would have recognized the double-play here. The English forms, *Presbyter* and *Priest* are both derived from the same Greek word, *presbuteros,* "elder," the former keeping the Greek form, *priest* coming from Latin through French. Those "elders" of the Presbyterian Church who had thrown off their Prelate Lord have in their turn become as bigoted and intolerant as the tyrants they once opposed. The sentence is intellectually brilliant, but we are not moved as we were in *Lycidas*.

Sonnet XV. To the Lord General Fairfax at the Siege of Colchester

This and the next are two of the sonnets Milton omitted from the edition of 1673 for obvious political reasons; they were not published until 1694. Sir Thomas Fairfax had proved himself a great military leader in various engagements throughout the Civil War, particularly at the Battles of Marston Moor and Naseby. Always in the thick of battle, he had impressed his men by his indomitable vigor and complete disregard for his personal safety. Peace, following the rout of the Royalists, had continued for two years when in 1648, the year of this sonnet, "new rebellions" raised their "Hydra heads," calling, as had the appearance of the legendary nine-headed monsters, for another Hercules. There were uprisings of Royalist troops in Wales and Kent, and at about the same time, the "false North," the Scots, invaded England in violation of the Solemn League and Covenant they had made with Parliament. Cromwell, after quelling the Welsh insurrection, moved north and defeated the Scots at the Battle of Preston. Fairfax took Maidstone and, when the Royalists strongly entrenched themselves in the walled town of Colchester, blockaded and besieged it until the Royalists were literally starved out and surrendered on August 27, 1648. Like all members of his party, Milton had reason to praise Fairfax's "firm unshaken virtue," a word used in both its moral sense and its more literal meaning of "manly strength." In this sonnet, unlike many of the others, Milton makes a sharp division between octave, devoted to praise of Fairfax's valor, and sestet, in which he turns from what Fairfax has already accomplished on the field, to warning of tasks that lie before him in the period of reconstruction that inevitably follows war. The sestet is unconsciously ironic, so far as Fairfax is concerned, since after his great triumph at Colchester, he passed into political obscurity. Although he continued to bear the title, Commander-in-Chief, military power passed imperceptibly from him to Cromwell. A year after his victory he retired from his military duties, and at no time took upon him duties of the State.

Milton was quite right in feeling that the situation of his party in England would be a parlous one, not to be finally settled by any amount of fighting on battle fields. "For what can war but endless war still breed"—Milton's generation had had no such drastic experience as has ours of the twentieth century, but it had learned, as must every generation torn by war,

> In vain doth valor bleed
> While avarice and rapine share the land.

Estates of Royalists had been confiscated, exorbitant financial penalties laid upon them, taxes were sharply rising, bribery, corruption and fraud were everywhere. The abuses were not limited to Royalists. The party in power was responsible for many of the burdens under which Puritans, too, were suffering almost as much as the enemy they had conquered. "O for that warning voice," Milton wrote in *Paradise Lost*. His function—and he felt it deeply in those days when his party was boasting of its triumph in battle—was to warn them that the real struggle lay ahead. No one can doubt the sincerity that rings through this sonnet and the next, which have much in common.

Sonnet XVI. To the Lord General Cromwell

This sonnet, as the long subtitle indicates, was written at a particular time for a specific purpose: "On the proposals of certain ministers at the Committee for Propagation of the Gospel." Such a committee had been appointed by Parliament in the spring of 1652 to consider the extent of toleration to be permitted in religious teaching outside the clergy. The members were specifically faced by a proposal of fifteen ministers, headed by John Owen who had been chaplain to Cromwell. From Milton's point of view, their proposals implied serious restrictions upon freedom of conscience, restrictions which he was right in thinking would involve still greater prohibitions as their authors continued to lay down limitations. Cromwell had so far opposed such measures, but Milton was aware that Cromwell might either not be willing or not be able to go as far in toleration as Milton wished him to go.

Unlike the tailed sonnet, this one would live even if we knew nothing of the particular circumstances that provoked it. It reflects Milton's reiterated warning to his party in *Areopagitica* and in some of the preceding sonnets, that the professed champions of liberty were in danger of imposing the very kind of bondage against which they had fought, and that "new Presbyter" was indeed likely to prove "old Priest writ large." As in the sonnet to Fairfax, the octave is devoted to praise, the sestet to warning and admonition, though octave and sestet are not arbitrarily divided here. In the octave Milton praises Cromwell, as he had praised Fairfax, for his past achievements. With "matchless fortitude" Cromwell, our "chief of men" had triumphantly led his country through war. All were aware of his great victories at the Battle of Preston on the banks of "Darwen stream," at Dunbar and at Worcester. Through every adversity he had plowed his way to peace and truth (1. 4). (Professor Merritt Hughes has called attention to an interesting double meaning in this line. The figures of Truth and Peace appeared upon a coin issued by Parliament in honor of Cromwell's victories at Preston, Dunbar and Worcester.) But across the well-justified praise, we hear again the note of admonition and warning: "yet much remains to conquer still." We have won the war, but will we win the peace? There are enemies who threaten our souls, as dangerous as any of those who on the field of battle threatened our bodies. The new foes will attempt to bind our souls with secular chains. Milton cries out to Cromwell to help England save the free conscience of true religion from the wolves —the figure recalls the one in *Lycidas* and will appear again in *Paradise Lost*—who threaten the sheep. The final couplet is used deliberately, as is the simple but intentionally ugly rhyme, "paw" and "maw"—mean words for base objects.

Sonnet XVII. To Sir Henry Vane the Younger

Sir Henry Vane (usually spoken of as "Young Sir Henry," because his father, "Old Sir Henry" was alive) was an important member of the Council and of Parliament, concerned with foreign affairs and the administration of the Navy. The duties of his office had become acute by the declaration of war between England and Holland. Milton sent a copy of this sonnet to Vane on July 3, 1652, three days after the Dutch ambassadors were dismissed from England. In the octave Milton is writing about these recent political developments and, as usual, thinking in terms of classical analogues. In his tribute to the statesman, he reminds him of the righteous firmness of the Roman Senate, which, even more than the valor of soldiers, defeated Pyrrhus, King of Epirus, "the fierce Epirot," and Hannibal, "the African bold." He feels sure that Vane will be capable of equal firmness, whether peace is declared or war continued with the "hollow states." Here Milton is punning upon the "hollow"—deceitful—character of the Dutch, and the "hollowness" of Holland, much of which lies below sea-level. In the sestet, beginning in the middle of a line, as so often, Milton passes from the immediate political issues, to what was always of paramount importance in his mind: the basic problems of liberty of conscience. Both Milton and Vane were among the Independents who insisted on the distinction between civil and ecclesiastical authority, making a sharp division between "the bounds of either sword." He is assured that Sir Henry Vane's firm hand will guide the state and will uphold the true religion.

Sonnet XVIII. On the Late Massacre in Piedmont

The outrage of the slaughter of the Piedmontese, by order of the Duke of Savoy on April 24, 1653, had shocked all Protestants. In their eyes, the Vaudois, or Waldensians, living quietly apart in an isolated section of the Alps, were true primitive Christians who for hundreds of years had kept alive the spirit of the teaching of Christ. Without warning they were set upon and slaughtered with every kind of barbarity. It is estimated that 1712 men, women and children were killed. The few fugitives who escaped over the wild and desolate snow-covered mountains carried word of the massacre to Paris, begging the protection of Protestants.

In his capacity as Latin Secretary, Milton, acting for Cromwell, wrote an official protest to the Duke of Savoy, followed by letters of state to the kings of Denmark, Sweden, to the Dutch Republic and the Swiss Protestant cantons, urging them to join the British Commonwealth in protest. Similar appeals were sent to Cardinal Mazarin and to the King of France. Cromwell also sent a special ambassador to Savoy to protest the persecution and to indicate that Cromwell was willing to go to war if necessary. From his state papers which, though firm and outspoken, nevertheless had to be restrained within the limits of international diplomacy, Milton turned to poetry for release of his profound emotion. In structure, style and intensity of feeling, this is Milton's greatest "trumpet."

Even Milton never so surpassed himself in keeping within the limitations of a form yet in releasing that form from the narrow restrictions it might have imposed. There is no line, with the possible exception of the second, at the end of which we pause as we read the sonnet aloud. Inevitably we are carried on through the first quatrain to find the governing verb, "Forget not." We cannot be sure whether the sestet begins in the eighth line with "Their moans" or in the tenth, with "Their martyred blood and ashes," nor does it matter, since octave and sestet are magnificently welded into one masterly whole.

In *Lycidas* alone has Milton so far achieved such majestic control over sound, meaning and structure. Here again we hear the smiting of that two-handed engine at the door—the prophecy of doom. The sheep in *Lycidas* died of sheep-rot, while their crass shepherds made raucous music, but the situation here is even more drastic. The Piedmontese had been the original sheep of the Good Shepherd; they had followed His gospel while our rude ancestors were still worshipping stocks and stones. As from the dragon's teeth once sprang up armed men, so from the martyred blood and ashes strewn over the fields of Italy will come retribution upon the "triple Tyrant." We cannot break this sonnet into artificial distinction of two themes, one in octave, another in sestet. It is all one great invective, calling for vengeance, from "Avenge, O Lord" to "Babylonian woe," the destruction foretold in the Apocalypse. In its compelling resonance (the sonnet must be read aloud) Milton continues the "dread voice" of the Old Testament, "Vengeance is mine" with the "loud voice" of Revelation, at the opening of the fifth seal, "How long, O Lord, holy and true, dost thou not judge and avenge our blood on them that dwell on the earth."

III

THE MAJOR POEMS

Paradise Lost

DEVELOPMENT

In "The Education of a Poet" we have found some indications that the youthful Milton aspired to write an epic. Indeed, during his second year at Cambridge, he tried his hand at a "little epic" in a Latin poem, "In Quintum Novembris." As the title implies, the poem was written for November 5, "Guy Fawkes' Day." Fawkes and eight other conspirators had plotted to blow up Parliament House on November 5, 1605, when James was present for the opening of Parliament. The plot was detected just in time. By order of Parliament, the day was to be forever memorialized by England. The universities always held formal exercises which, at Cambridge, had produced such poems as Milton attempted, written in part under the influence of the "Spenserians," Giles and Phineas Fletcher, Cambridge dons, who had set the fashion. Milton's Latin exercise vaguely foreshadows *Paradise Lost,* in that its main character is Satan. Satan, jealous of the blessings he finds in England, speeds to Italy to urge the Pope to action against English heretics, then calls a council of devils in Hell to make his own plans—presumably to instigate the Gunpowder Plot. At the end of the poem, God, looking down from Heaven, laughs—as on three occasions God laughs in *Paradise Lost*—foreknowing how frustrate these diabolic plans will be. Two years later, however, in the "Vacation Exercise," Milton indicated that he intended to write his epic not in Latin but in his native language. The references in the Exercise and in the Sixth Elegy, naturally vague, suggest that his chief model was to be the *Odyssey,* but do not indicate any particular epic theme.

During the Horton years Milton must have given a good deal of thought to the project, while he was training himself in many different kinds of English verse. His ideas seem to have crystallized during his Italian travels, perhaps because his acquaintance with Manso seemed to bring him closer to Tasso, the Italian poet of epic in the vernacular, whose theory and practise were very influential on Milton. In the Latin verses he addressed to Manso, Milton, after paying high tribute to Italian literature, patriotically declares that the English, too, are votaries of Phoebus Apollo, and suggests that he himself has in mind an English epic. That the plan is still only tentative is implied in the Latin construction with which he introduces it: "si quando": "If ever I shall summon back our native kings into our songs, and Arthur, waging his wars beneath the earth, or if ever I shall proclaim the magnanimous heroes of the table . . ." Milton had apparently begun to think of an epic based upon King Arthur and the knights of the Round Table.

Milton's statement in the *Epitaphium Damonis* suggests that he had gone farther with his plans and was only waiting to discuss them with Diodati: "I, for my part, am resolved to tell the story of the Trojan ships in the Rutupian sea and of the ancient kingdom of Inogene." The *Iliad* and the *Aeneid* were to come home to British shores. Milton apparently intended to begin his epic with the coming of the Trojan fleet to England under Brutus, who married Inogene. Homer, Virgil and Spenser come together, since Spenser, too, had treated some of the themes Milton suggests. This would have been Milton's *Arthuriad,* in which, as Virgil had glorified Rome, Milton would sing the great past of Britain and her still greater future.

The plan was still in his mind when Milton set down about one hundred possible subjects for a major work in the Trinity or Cambridge manuscript. Among the thirty-three subjects from British history, Arthurian materials are mentioned. All the subjects in the Trinity manuscript are for dramas, but it is probable that Milton made another list for epics, which has not been preserved. That he continued his plans for an *Arthuriad* until at least 1642 is shown in his prose works. In the *Apology for Smectymnuus,* Milton speaks of stages in his early reading and interests: after "grave orators and historians," "the smooth elegiac poets," and "the two famous renowners of Beatrice and Laura," he mentions as another path "whither my younger feet wandered," "those lofty fables and romances, which recount in solemn cantos the deed of knighthood founded by our victorious kings." In another passage, often quoted from the *Reason of Church Government,* Milton describes the task he had set himself for writing three major works. One is in "that epic form whereof the two poems of Homer and those other two of Virgil and Tasso, are a diffuse, and the book of Job a brief, model." His mind is still on an English epic, since he adds: "and lastly, what king or knight before the conquest might be chosen in whom to lay the pattern of a Christian hero."

Just when and why Milton gave up the idea of an *Arthuriad* remains a matter of surmise. The subjects in the Trinity manuscript suggest that he had been reading British history. A little later he began to devote his spare time to his *History of Britain.* Certainly by that time he had come to question the authenticity of the Arthurian story, since he raises the question whether any such person as Arthur ever reigned in England. Such a doubt would have been sufficient grounds for Milton to discard the idea of an *Arthuriad,* since basic to his conception of the function of a poet was the fact that the poet must deal with *truth.* Something of this growing doubt is implied in the Prologue to Book IX of *Paradise Lost,* where he mentioned among materials he had dismissed, "fabled knights, In battles feigned," and other trappings of chivalry, which, he says with some contempt, are "not that which justly gives heroic name To person or to poem."

Even if Milton had not given up the idea of an *Arthuriad* fairly early in his middle years, it seems inevitable that he would have done so as his political career developed, not so much for lack of time as for his changing attitude to the party he had once believed would bring about a glorious England. He had reached a point in his study of history when he could no longer believe in the authenticity of Arthur and England's reputed great past. He had reached a point, too, when he could hardly have prophesied the great future he had once envisioned for his country.

When, then, did he begin to write *Paradise Lost* as an epic? That question too can be answered only by surmise. We know that he had planned a drama on the Fall of Man well before he changed to an epic. For this we have the evidence both of the Trinity manuscript and of Milton's nephew, Edward Phillips, who said in his *Life* of his uncle: "This subject was first designed a tragedy, and in the fourth book of the poem there are six verses, which several years before the poem was begun, were shown to me and some others, as designed for the very beginning of the said tragedy." Phillips then quoted Satan's address to the sun (IV. 32-41). Phillips does not date his reminiscence, which Hanford and others give as "circa 1642." A legend has grown up that Phillips heard his uncle read the lines when he was still a schoolboy under his direction, but there is no evidence for this in Phillips' own words. He merely says, "Several years before the poem was begun." The passage that follows implies that Milton began the actual writing of *Paradise Lost* as an epic after he became blind. Phillips seems to have acted as a sort of editor-in-chief for his uncle. He says that he "had the perusal of it from the very beginning," and that for some years he read "parcels" of it—ten, twenty, thirty lines at a time—"which being written by whatever hand came next" often needed correction "as to the orthography and pointing"— that is, spelling and punctuation. This sounds as if Milton had been dependent from the beginning on a succession of amanuenses.

A majority of the subjects in the Trinity manuscript are Biblical. Of all the subjects, Milton seemed most interested in the Fall of Man. Four drafts appear in the manuscript, the first two listing only the characters, the third including a prologue, with a brief outline

of speakers and speeches, in five acts. The fourth, "Adam Unparadised," is a fairly complete scenario of the action, again in
five acts. Each draft includes a chorus. In the first three drafts we
notice more allegorial than real figures: Wisdom, Justice, Mercy,
Conscience, Sickness, Death and others, suggest the kind of masque-
figures in which Milton showed interest in his early poems. Perhaps
some vestiges of these early plans still remain in *Paradise Lost* in
the allegory of Sin and Death, and the suggestion of dumb-show and
pantomime of Death and Sickness in Michael's prophecies in
Book XI.

Let us assume that Milton actually wrote "Adam Unparadised,"
in part or in entirety as a drama. He might have done so in the
early 1640's while he still had comparative leisure, good health
and sight. When he returned to the theme, presumably in blindness, after he had been relieved of the heavier duties of his Secre-
taryship, why did he develop the materials into an epic? More interesting still, what sections of the original drama may still be
found in the epic?

The second question may be answered more easily than the first.
The scenario of "Adam Unparadised" opens with a prologue in
which the Angel Gabriel describes Paradise. The Chorus com-
ments on his coming to keep watch because of Lucifer's rebellion.
Gabriel tells of the creation of Adam and Eve, their love and marriage. Some such conversations occur in *Paradise Lost,* although
the speakers are changed. In Book V Raphael, rather than Michael, comes down to Eden (of which there are various descriptions in Book IV and elsewhere), tells Adam of Satan's rebellion
and of the Creation. Adam in turn describes his memories of his
own creation and of that of Eve.

In the third division of the scenario, Lucifer appears, "bemoans
himself; seeks revenge upon Man." The Chorus sings of the victory in Heaven, and also a hymn of the Creation. We find the section mentioned by Phillips in Satan's soliloquy in Book IV, the
warfare in Heaven in Book VI and the angelic hymn on Creation
in Book VII.

In the next act of the drama, Adam and Eve appear after the Fall, accusing each other. These speeches may well have been incorporated into the scene at the end of Book XI. At the end of the scene, the Chorus bewails Adam's Fall, as the angels mourn it in Book XI. In the last act of the scenario, Adam and Eve continue to accuse each other—as in Book XI—until Justice and the Chorus both admonish Adam. The Angel is sent to banish them from Paradise, "but, before, causes to pass before his eyes, in shapes, a masque of all the evils of this life and world." Here may be part of Book XI in which Michael shows a pageant of the future which begins with dumb-show before it becomes a series of scenes from Biblical history. It is entirely possible, then, that a series of "parcels," as Phillips called them, might have been picked up without much change from the drama and may now lie embedded in the epic.

But the most magnificent parts of *Paradise Lost* were not in the drama at all. Satan and his fallen legions in Hell, the great Council Scene in Pandemonium, Satan's voyage through space were not in the dramatic version. The scenes in Heaven in Book III are not there, nor do God or Christ appear as actors in "Adam Unparadised." The earlier Adam and Eve of Book IV do not appear, though their marriage is described, and the Chorus might conceivably have sung the Epithalamion, "Hail, wedded love!" Since Adam and Eve appear in the drama only after the Fall, the tenderest of their scenes together, as well as their long conversation with Raphael, are lacking. Let us put it this way: most of the scenes and speeches that make *Paradise Lost* memorable to us could not have been contained within the confines of a classical tragedy. We begin to have a clue to the answer to the first question: why did Milton write or rewrite his Fall of Man in epic form?

Milton would inevitably have found the unity of time impossible for full depiction of his characters and theme. Unless Adam and Eve fell on the very day of their creation (there is exegetical authority for such interpretation), nothing earlier than the Fall itself could have been depicted. There was little possibility of explaining why Adam and Eve fell, or why Satan rebelled and degenerated, within the limitation of a drama. The unity of time adds to the greatness of the Biblical drama upon which Milton finally decided. The last day of Samson's life proved the climax of his whole career, ethically, artistically, dramatically. But Adam and Eve, and particularly Satan, as Milton came to imagine them, could be restricted within no such limitation. ҆ we read *Paradise Lost* and watch the art with which Milton ҆s Satan' ҆egeneration and as we come to know Adam an ҆e before and after the Fall, we shall better understand why Milton freed himself from the unity of time.

Was there any advantage Milton might have had in "Adam Unparadised" that he lost by making the Fall of Man epic rather than drama? Various critics of *Paradise Lost* will say, *yes*. In the drama God and Christ did not appear as characters, and many critics feel that Milton would have been wiser not to make them actors in *Paradise Lost*. These are problems which we may consider further as we read the version of "Adam Unparadised" that became *Paradise Lost*.

BOOK I

The Prologue

There are four prologues in *Paradise Lost*—to Books I, III, VII, IX. Perhaps Satan's address to the sun in Book IV is another, but if so, it is deliberately in reverse to the plan of the others, all of which follow a pattern established in the general prologue. Following classical example, Milton took for granted that the epic poet would at once state the theme of his work and invoke a Muse. Homer began the *Iliad* (in Pope's translation)

> Achilles' wrath, to Greece the direful spring
> Of woes unnumbered, Heavenly Goddess, sing!

The Muse of the Odyssey was asked to sing of the wanderings of long-tried Odysseus. Virgil opened the *Aeneid,* with the words, "Arma virumque cano" (Arms and the man I sing). Milton states the subject of *Paradise Lost* as "man's first disobedience." Notice that the emphasis is upon *Man,* not upon Satan, who is not mentioned in the Prologue and not referred to until line 34. Milton is following his classical ancestors not only in the immediate introduction of his chief subject but in the grammatical structure, which is highly Latinate. We do not know the construction of the first phrase until line 6, when we find it in, "Sing, Heavenly Muse."

The prologue shows clearly that the subject matter will be taken from the first chapters of Genesis: the disobedience of Man in eating the fruit of the tree of the knowledge of good and evil, and his Fall as a consequence, bringing death into the world, and all the woes from which Man has continued to suffer. But we should notice that, although the story begins with the man who fell, it also mentions the "greater Man" Who will redeem us. The significance of this, we shall understand later in *Paradise Lost.*

The invocation to a Muse is a classical device, and in later prologues, Milton will give his Muse a classical name, Urania, goddess of astronomy, a fitting choice for a poem leading to Heaven. Here, however, she is called "Heavenly Muse," and is localized not, as she might have been by Homer or Virgil, upon Mount Olympus or Mount Helicon, but "on the secret top" of Horeb, Sinai, sacred in Hebraic belief, associated here particularly with Moses,

> That shepherd who first taught the chosen seed
> In the beginning how the Heavens and earth
> Rose out of Chaos.

Since a Muse was invoked by a classical poet to aid him in what he was attempting to write, Milton asks his Muse to lead him higher than the "Aonian mount" of the classical poets, since the subject of his epic is "higher" than theirs. Here our memories may go back to *Lycidas* where on two occasions we heard a strain of a "higher mood," as Christianity rose above the pagan tradition. The prologues in *Paradise Lost* begin as classical invocations, but, with one exception, they rise to Christian prayers to the Holy Spirit, read by Christians into the second verse of Genesis: "and the Spirit of God moved upon the face of the waters."

> Thou from the first
> Wast present, and with mighty wings outspread,
> Dove-like satst brooding on the vast Abyss
> And madst it pregnant.

Milton's prologues are the more poignant in that, in addition to the problems implied by every poet who invoked his Muse for aid, Milton was always conscious of his greatest limitation—his blindness. In other prologues he will refer to it more specifically. Here it is suggested only in, "What in me is dark, Illumine:"

> That to the height of this great argument
> I may assert Eternal Providence,
> And justify the ways of God to men.

In twenty-six lines, we have learned the theme of *Paradise Lost,* "man's first disobedience"; we know that the materials are to be drawn chiefly from Genesis, that Milton is writing a classical epic, but that he intends, with the aid of the "Heavenly Muse" to transcend the classical, and in a poem both Hebrew and Christian, deal with the most profound of all problems, "to justify the ways of God to men." In twenty-six lines Milton has fused three great civilizations, the main sources of Renaissance religious poetry: classical, Hebrew, Christian. (I suggest that the student read at this point the first section of Gilbert Murray, *The Classical Tradition in Poetry:* in which Mr. Murray analyzes in close detail these twenty-six lines, showing how they reflect the classical tradition.)

The Degeneration of Satan

With Blake, Shelley, Byron, the "Satanic School" of Milton criticism began to develop. Milton, said Blake, was of the devil's party, whether he knew it or not; Satan is the hero of *Paradise Lost*. The idea had been suggested as early as Dryden, though not so vividly expressed as by the later writers. It is easy to understand why such an interpretation would appeal to Romanticists, rebels in various ways, who sympathized with the fact that Milton, too, had been a rebel, allying himself with the party that put a king to death. It is probably true that Milton's position in regard to the authority of kingship made him more capable of understanding the First Great Rebel than a Cavalier might have been, but we must constantly be on guard against over-reading any author's biography or personal character into his works. Whether Shakespeare was Hamlet or not, he was certainly not always and not only Hamlet. The "Satanists" did not prove Satan the hero of *Paradise Lost*. They could not. When I discover tendencies to "Satanism" among my students (many of whom do not know that there ever was such a school) I usually find that they have read no farther than Books I and II of *Paradise Lost,* the books usually excerpted in anthologies. Had Blake and Shelley and Byron, I wonder, read Book X?

The character of Satan is one of the greatest creations in any language. The greatness lies not only—indeed, not primarily—in the depiction of the majestic character of Books I and II, but in the slow and steady degeneration of an angel who once stood next to God Himself in Heaven. As we read *Paradise Lost* we watch the subtlety of Milton's art as the character gradually diminishes from grandeur and magnificence to baseness and final degradation, so that we are inevitably alienated from admiration. In following the degeneration of Satan, we must realize that Milton is, as always in *Paradise Lost,* writing on two levels, a literal and a moral. On the literal level, Satan is a character, a person, about whom a story is woven. Milton's basic technique is a subtle change in figures of speech, mutation of the images to which Satan is compared. Let me sketch this technique in general so that you may have the pleasure of watching it for yourself as you accustom yourself to noticing carefully each comparison Milton makes.

The first physical attribute of Satan as he emerges from the burning lake and made toward the shore is his tremendous size. As he moves toward shore, we are still more conscious of physical size. Following classical tradition, Milton does not describe him in detail but emphasizes two objects he carries. His shield, Milton compares (I. 284-291) to the largest round object human eyes had ever seen, the moon seen through Galileo's telescope. His spear (I. 292-294) is so gigantic that the tallest pine tree, used for the mast of a flagship, seems only a wand in comparison. On the basis of that shield and spear, our imaginations begin to frame the gigantic stature of this Titan. After the commander-in-chief has brought order out of the chaos into which his army had fallen, Satan stands reviewing them. Now he is like a proud tower, then like the sun (I. 591, 594). In the sun-figure, we see what Milton's technique will be. Satan has not yet lost all the original brightness of an angel in heaven, for he still may be compared with the sun and moon. But some of the glory has been lost, for he is like the sun seen through morning mist, or like moon in eclipse. The sun through a mist, the moon in eclipse, but still the sun and moon. So Satan continues for some time, majestic, grand, yet always a little more flawed. After his extraordinary voyage in Book II, when he "holds gladly the port," he is compared with a ship with "shrouds and tackle torn." (II. 1043-44) One of the last occasions that Milton uses a grand comparison for Satan is the scene at the end of Book IV in which the angelic squadrons begin to hem Satan round and he turns upon them with all the courage he still possesses:

> On the other side Satan, alarmed,
> Collecting all his might, dilated stood,

Like Teneriffe or Atlas, unremoved:
His stature reached the sky, and on his crest
Sat Horror plumed.

(IV. 985-989)

Earlier in the same book, we have had evidence that the figures
of speech are changing. When Satan is seeking entrance to the
Garden of Eden, he disdains the gate and leaps over the wall. As in
Lycidas, Milton thinks of Satan as "a prowling wolf" leaping over
the fence into the sheepfold, as a thief, forcing his way through sub-
stantial doors for plunder. "So clomb this first grand Thief into
God's fold."

In Book IV the analogues are largely animal-imagery. After
Satan has entered Eden, he chooses as his vantage point a tree on
which he "sat like a cormorant." (IV. 196) Later in that book, he
is like a "proud steed reined," "champing his iron curb." (IV. 857-
59) When Satan begins the temptation of Eve through her dream, he
is "squat like a toad," a grotesque and almost comic figure. His potential greatness is still there, however, for as Ithuriel touches him
with his spear:

Up he starts,
Discovered and surprised. As, when a spark
Lights on a heap of nitrous powder, laid
Fit for the tun, some magazine to store
Against a rumored war, the smutty grain,
With sudden blaze diffused, inflames the air,
So started up, in his own shape, the Fiend.

(IV. 813-19)

The momentary blaze of glory does not obscure the danger of
Satan, the spark that ignites gunpowder stored for war.

When the comparisons are with birds, they are with the cormorant or the vulture, which far off seem both grand and magnificent, but which are carrion birds of prey. More and more the
analogues are with low things. In his search of the serpent

> through each thicket dank or dry,
> Like a black mist, low-creeping, he held on
> His midnight search.
>
> (IX. 179-181)

Subconsciously we are prepared for that climactic scene in Book X in which he becomes the snake he has permitted himself to be.

In the meantime, we watch a degeneration in Satan's moral character parallel to the changes in his physical appearance. I shall not anticipate the pleasure the reader will have in studying this for himself, except by giving one clue and explaining one key-word, whose meaning might not at first be clear. The moral degeneration of Satan is suggested in part by Milton's subtle changes in figures of light and darkness. When he was an angel in Heaven, Satan, like God and the other angels, had been clothed in light. Even in the early scenes in which he is still majestic, he is losing some of his original brightness. Watch this in the scene in which, having aroused his followers, the great commander brings his fallen army to order, and reviews them, as a general his troops. (I. 587-619). We never feel the contrast between what he was and what he is permitting himself to become more than in this poignant scene. In the later books, as Satan deliberately continues to choose evil rather than good, light gives way more and more to darkness.

The first dangerous quality of Satan emphasized by Milton is "obdurate Pride" (I. 58), which proves his besetting sin. The word is repeated again and again. To modern readers Pride often seems an admirable quality, but we must understand the word as did Milton and his contemporaries. From their classical ancestors, they had inherited a conception of Hybris (the Greek word for Pride) as a dangerous quality. Many of the most familiar stories of classical mythology were based upon the belief that Hybris was the sin most frequently punished by the gods. The idea is a reiterated motif in classical tragedy, as well as in legend. In addition to this was the Christian emphasis upon meekness and humility, according to which Pride was the most deadly of the Seven Deadly Sins. Later in our study, when we come to consider the idea of "hierarchy," as Milton and his contemporaries understood it, we shall find the belief that, as all things were created in the universe, they were established in "degree" and "order" in a scale or ladder of Nature, a great chain of being (there were many different phrases in which the idea was expressed). In that scale, ladder or chain, men and angels all had ranks or degrees. As they were created, so they should be content to remain. Classical and Christian teachers combined in their warning to man to be content, not to aspire for a higher place, not to permit himself to fall to a lower rank. Pope put the time-honored ethical belief into couplets in the *Essay on Man,* among them these:

> In Pride, in reas'ning Pride our error lies;
> All quit their spheres, and rush into the skies.
> Pride still is aiming at the blest abodes,
> Men would be angels, angels would be gods.
> Aspiring to be gods, if angels fell,
> Aspiring to be angels, men rebel.
>
> (*Essay on Man,* I. 123-28)

Pope said, again, as Raphael will warn Adam in Book VIII of *Paradise Lost:*

> The bliss of man (could Pride the blessing find)
> Is not to think or act beyond mankind.
>
> (I. 189-90)

"Know thy own point" is the lesson of the *Essay on Man,* echoing centuries of the teaching of such ethics. Do not break the chain of being: "Whatever link you strike, Tenth or tenth thousandth, breaks the chain alike." Satan, we shall learn, deliberately broke the chain of being. Listen for the word "Pride," frequently reiterated, watch the increasing obduracy of Satan, his persistent refusal to choose right, his deliberate choice of evil, with his accompanying physical and moral degeneration.

Epic Figures of Speech

A favorite figure, inherited by Renaissance poets from their classical ancestors, was the "Homeric simile." If we stop over an example in Book I, the student will easily learn to recognize such figures and analyze them for himself. Let us take the first extended description of Satan (I. 192-210), emphasizing his gigantic size. We see Satan still lying on the lava-lake, his head "uplift above the wave," the rest of his body

> Prone on the flood extended, long and huge
> Lay floating many a rood.

Briefly he is compared first to the legendary Titans, then at much more length to the Leviathan of Psalm CIV. 26, "which God of all His works Created hugest." In a Homeric simile we start with a comparison between A (Satan) and B (Leviathan) but the second member grows until it eclipses the first. Milton develops old mariners' "fish stories" of a sea-creature larger even than the whale, which had been often mistaken by pilots for an island against which they tried to moor their boats. Only after eight lines of such detail do we return to A: "So stretched out, huge in length, the Arch-Fiend lay."

Milton is a master of similes, Homeric and others. We find one of the finest sequences in Book I, showing how deftly the artist chose his comparisons to produce his effects. After Satan and Beelzebub have roused from stunned unconsciousness and reached the shore, the other fallen angels still lie stupefied upon the burning lake. Only at the sound of the clarion-voice of their commander do they begin to rouse from lethargy. Watch carefully each of Milton's similes in the long passage (ll. 301-360). All the comparisons have one thing in common: the fallen angels are innumerable. The Bible had said that "a third part" of the angels fell with Lucifer, but neither Satan nor Milton knew how many angels had originally been in Heaven.

In the first simile two aspects are emphasized: the *vast number* and the *confusion*. Milton's mind went back to his Italian journey for the first comparison. The angels lay, "Thick as autumnal leaves that strew the brooks in Vallombrosa." Anyone who has scuffed through autumn leaves knows how numberless they seem, but in Vallombrosa ("shady valley"), famous district of woods and forests near Florence, they were even more impressive than in England. In the second figure Milton's imagination goes back to one of the most familiar stories in the Old Testament, the passage of the Israelites through the Red Sea, pursued by Pharaoh, whose chariots and horsemen were destroyed and lay floating confusedly in the waves that closed behind the chosen people. Again we have the sense of confusion and an uncounted number of carcasses and chariots. And notice (as in *Lycidas*) the underlying water-imagery of brooks in Vallambrosa and the Red Sea, appropriate because the fallen angels are still lying on the lake.

At Satan's call, "Awake, arise; or be forever fallen" the legions begin to rouse from stupor. Again there are two comparisons, one brief, one more Homeric. The first, appropriate for fallen soldiers, is to sentinels asleep on duty. Then Milton goes back again to the Bible in the more expanded comparison of the fallen angels to the plague of locusts called up by Moses, that "o'er the realm of impious Pharaoh hung Like night, and darkened all the land of Nile." Again the angels are numberless (1.344) and again the comparison is with an unnumbered throng of flying pests that descended upon the land. First stupefied on the lake, then flying upon their wings, the legions of Satan reach the shore. In the third series of figures, an ordered army begins to emerge from chaos, (I. 347ff.) but not before Milton introduces one more figure emphasizing untold numbers and the sense of confusion among the fallen angels, whose swarming down to earth is like the descent of the barbarians upon Rome:

A multitude like which the populous North
Poured never from her frozen loins, to pass
Rhine or the Danube, when her barbarous sons
Came like a deluge on the South.

(I. 351-54)

Notice one other matter of craft in this masterly passage of figures
of speech. With the exception of the autumn leaves and the sentinels, the comparisons—like those in the degeneration of Satan
—have been with things dangerous and destructive—the carcasses
and chariots in the Red Sea, symbols of destroyers who were destroyed, the pitchy cloud of locusts that blotted out the sun from
the earth, the barbarians from the north who strove to destroy
the grandeur that was Rome.

Milton's Hells

It is a misnomer to talk about "Milton's Hell." There are at least
three distinct physical Hells in *Paradise Lost* in addition to the ethical or moral Hell that gives unity to all of them. Basically the first
Hell is a place of darkness which the lurid flickering light of fire
serves only to make more dark. (ll. 62 ff.) Geologically, it is a volcanic region, "fed With ever-burning sulphur unconsumed." Satan
and his followers have fallen into a "fiery gulf," a lake that burns
continually with "liquid fire." The beach of that "inflamed sea"
marks the beginning of a "dreary plain, forlorn and wild." When
Satan "rears from off the pool His mighty stature," he flies to what
seems dry land

if it were land that ever burned
With solid, as the lake with liquid fire.

(I. 228-229)

The land proves to be "firm brimstone," but the heat is as intense
as was that of the boiling pool, with the result that Satan walks

delicately with "uneasy steps Over the burning marl." Heat is everywhere in "the torrid clime . . . vaulted with fire." In the background, we learn, is a volcanic mountain:

> There stood a hill not far, whose grisly top
> Belched fire and rolling smoke; the rest entire
> Shone with a glossy scurf—undoubted sign
> That in his womb was hid metallic ore,
> The work of sulphur.
>
> (I. 670-674)

While there are both classical and medieval analogues to other aspects of Milton's first Hell, those I have been emphasizing are different from the traditional and familiar elements, and lead me to believe that Milton was drawing upon visual memory as well as upon imagination and combining actual sense impressions with literary reminiscence. In his blindness, I think that his memory went back to an occasion during his Italian journey when he had visited the Phlegraean Fields, lying close to Naples, near which the Puteoli villa of Manso was situated. This extraordinary volcanic district was usually a part of the traveller's tour and particularly impressed English visitors who had nothing in their own country to correspond to the strange sight. While Milton did not specifically refer to a visit to the Phlegraean Fields, it would have been almost inconceivable that he should not have visited a place with so many legendary and literary associations. For centuries this district had been considered the locale of the early battles between the gods and giants. It was also said to be the dwelling place of Homer's "sunless Cimmerians" who lived in perpetual darkness around the Lake of Avernus, across which no bird might safely fly. Its great crater was the entrance to Hades, through which Aeneas and others descended to the infernal regions. Apart from legend, it had many literary associations. It was said that Virgil's spirit often appeared there, hovering about his sepulchral urn near the Grotto Vecchia, close by his villa on the Pausilypon. Cicero's villa was not far from Avernus, and at Puteoli St. Paul had spent seven days on his journey to Rome.

The topographical similarities between the Phlegraean Fields and Milton's first Hell are striking even today. The Solfatara—called in ancient times the Forum Vulcani—is the crater of a half-extinct volcano, destitute of vegetation; on the right, there is still a pool of hot water; other pools have formed and disappeared. The "dreary plain" around the lake is still as hot as when Satan and his companions walked with uneasy steps over the burning marl. But a volcanic district is not static. Hills are thrown up, depressions and pools change their places. The most spectacular change in the Phlegraean Fields occurred in 1538 when a mountain—Monte Nuovo—appeared almost overnight.

Fortunately—for my theory at least—we have a first-hand account of the appearance of the district in 1638, the year of Milton's visit to Naples, by one of the greatest living experts of that day on volcanoes and earthquakes, Athanasius Kircher, a Jesuit priest of wide scientific interests. Kircher described the entrance through a dark grotto into "a Plain altogether formidable and full of horror." The soil, he said, "sounds and rattles like a Drum . . . and you may feel boiling waters under your feet." Most of all, the boiling lake amazed him. "Yet an huge Laky-ditch in the same Plain did wonderfully affect me. For it is found full of boiling waters, and ready to fright one with their blackness." Kircher's conclusion to his long and detailed account in the *Mundus Subterraneus* is significant of the impression made by the district on an observer more travelled and much more familiar with volcanic districts than the young Milton had been: "You would think yourself almost in the midst of Hell; where all things appear horrid, sad and lamentable, with a most formidable face of things." *

* In my article on this subject, "Milton's Hell and the Phlegraean Fields (*U.T.Q.* VII [1938] 500-513), I included two contemporary pictures, one from Kircher's account, and one from George Sandys, *Relation of a Journey* with some of the descriptions given by Sandys, whose book seems to have been a sort of "Baedeker" for the region.

H

Milton's Second Hell

At the end of Book I (ll. 670-798) we watch the building of
Pandemonium, the second Hell. The word "Pandemonium" in
Book I, implies simply that it is a place of "all devils or demons."
Not until Book X does it take on the connotation of "confusion"
with which we associate it today. Although I have suggested, in
the article referred to above, passing similarities with the accounts
of Kircher and Sandys, these are not very significant, and certainly
far less important than two other sources. On the one hand, the
building of Pandemonium is the work of human—or angelic—
hands. The architect, we learn (ll. 732-750) was a fallen angel
who in times to come would become the architect Mulciber
(Greek, *Hephaestus,* Roman, *Vulcan*). The work was performed
under the direction of Mammon by artisans and craftsmen who
like "bands Of pioneers, with spade and pick axe armed. . . .
Rifled the bowels of their mother earth For treasures better hid."
(ll. 678-688) But in addition to the art and craft of fallen angels,
magic is implied in

> Anon out of the earth a fabric huge
> Rose like an exhalation, with the sound
> Of dulcet symphonies and voices sweet.

> (I. 710-712)

Here the ears of some modern critics catch echoes of a masque
presented at court on Sunday after Twelfth Night in 1637 (three
years after the production of *Comus*), in which the "spectacle" was
of the opening of the earth and the rising of a "richly adorned
pallace, seeming all of goldsmith's work." Details of vaulted porti-
cos, pilasters and "capitels of gold" are very similar to the details
of Pandemonium. (For more complete details see Merritt Hughes'
note on this passage, p. 229).

Even more striking are parallels between Pandemonium and St.

Peter's Cathedral in Rome, which persuade me that here, as in the first Hell, Milton's visual memory merged with literary traditions. No English traveller of the seventeenth century, no matter what his religion, could fail to be impressed by St. Peter's, the largest and most magnificent building he had ever seen. While St. Peter's was still unfinished when Milton visited Rome, all the details mentioned in the description of Pandemonium were there. Many years ago one of my students at the University ot Chicago studied all the pictures and plates she could find by contemporary architects and engravers and pointed out the striking similarities between the architecture of St. Peter's and that of Pandemonium. (Rebecca W. Smith, "The Source of Milton's Pandemonium.") A more recent student, Mrs. Margaret Byard, added still more details in an unpublished seminar paper at Columbia University. The pilasters, architrave, cornices, sculptures, pillars were all there, though the pillars of St. Peter's are Corinthian, not Doric, as in Pandemonium. Both the cathedral and Pandemonium were lighted by "starry lamps and blazing cressets." One of the things that most impressed visitors to St. Peter's was the immense size of the doors, in comparison with which human beings seem to shrink into insignificance. So Milton suggests when his fallen angels—giants though they are—are compared first with bees swarming about a hive, then with other puny and tiny creatures:

> So thick the airy crowd
> Swarmed and were straitened; till, the signal given,
> Behold a wonder! they but now who seemed
> In bigness to surpass Earth's giant sons,
> Now less than smallest dwarfs, in narrow room
> Throng numberless, like that Pygmean race
> Beyond the Indian mount, or fairy elves. . . .
> Thus incorporeal spirits to smallest forms
> Reduced their shapes immense, and were at large,
> Though without number still, amidst the hall
> Of that infernal court.
>
> (I. 775-792)

Most striking of all the similarities between Pandemonium and St. Peter's is the fact that there is evidently another building close by Pandemonium. While the hosts of lesser angels throng into the temple, Satan, Beelzebub and the other more important angels enter a council chamber apparently attached to but somehow separate from the Cathedral. This is obviously the Vatican, the library of which we know Milton visited when he was in Rome. The closing lines of Book I and the first part of Book II must be read on two levels of meaning. In addition to the literal story on the surface, another level begins to be implied in these lines:

> But far within,
> And in their own dimensions, like themselves,
> The great Seraphic Lords and Cherubim
> In close recess and secret conclave sat—
> A thousand demi-gods on golden seats,
> Frequent and full. After short silence, then,
> And summons read, the great consult began.
>
> (I. 792-99)

"Close recess" and "secret conclave" were phrases Protestants liked to throw at Roman Catholics. Book II opens with a description of the throne, which is not only the throne usurped by Satan, but the papal throne in the Vatican. It is interesting to know, in connection with the figure of the bees Milton used, that bees were the emblems of the Barberini Pope Urban VIII, who dedicated St. Peter's, and that his followers were frequently called "bees." The Council scene in Book II, in addition to its many classical reminiscences, is on the other level of meaning, Milton's Protestant parody of the election of a Pope by the College of Cardinals in "close recess and secret conclave."

Milton's Third Hell

The two Hells discussed so far are very different. In spite of the
fact that, during the council, some of the speakers refer to the discomforts of the Hell into which they have fallen, it is clear that Pandemonium is not only magnificent but very comfortable indeed—
the Belial party is quite willing to stay there indefinitely—and that
the fallen angels seem to forget the smoke and stench and fire they
first encountered. Perhaps the unnamed architect of Pandemonium
was the father of modern air-conditioning! But the first two hells
are alike in that they occupy a limited area. In the passage beginning in II. 750, however, we are given a quite different conception of the size of Hell. After the council has disbanded, some of
the angels take part in Olympic games of celebration. One group of
angels, inquiring Renaissance spirits as they are, set out to explore
their new domain and find that Hell is not a limited part of a world,
but a world in itself. Parts of it are very hot, as the angels had already discovered, but parts are as intensely cold. There is "a frozen continent" with perpetual storms, with hail that never melts.
But Hell is much more than a continent: it is a world, topographi-
cally much like our own world, with rivers and seas, with mountains and valleys, with a "gulf profound" into which whole armies
might have sunk:

> Thus roving on
> In confused march forlorn, the adventurous bands
> With shuddering horror pale, and eyes aghast,
> Viewed first their lamentable lot, and found
> No rest. Through many a dark and dreary vale
> They passed, and many a region dolorous,
> O'er many a frozen, many a fiery Alp,
> Rockes, caves, lakes, fens, bogs, dens and shades of death.
>   (II. 614-621)

In addition to many other sources that went to the making of this passage, I have suggested (*Science and Imagination,* pp. 78-9) the possibility that Milton may be reflecting here the picture of the new world in the moon drawn by Johann Kepler in his *Somnium,* a description so graphic that, once read, it cannot be forgotten. There is something of the combined grandeur and grotesqueness of Kepler's picture here. Milton's third Hell, like Kepler's moon, is a place of "fierce extremes, extremes by change more fierce." Its cold is colder than anything on earth, its heat more torrid. As Milton says, "the parching air Burns frore, and cold performs the effect of fire." Milton's frozen world in Hell is much like Kepler's. Kepler's lunar mountains, too, tower to vast heights, and his caverns and fissures on the moon are as profound as Milton's Serbonian bog. But I shall not labor these comparisons, which I do not attempt to prove but merely to suggest. The important thing is not the source of the third Hell, but the fact that Milton's Hell is no such limited and constricted place as Satan and his fallen angels first believed when they roused from their stupor on the burning lake.

The Catalogue of Fallen Angels

We remember that, as early as the *Nativity Ode,* Milton had shown a great deal of interest in demonology, and had called a lesser roll of demons, stressing the fact that many of them were worshiped under various titles by Phoenicians and Assyrians, appearing with more familiar names in Greece and Rome. In Book I of *Paradise Lost* (ll. 376-521) Milton summons before us a much more extensive band of demons. He was following here a familiar pattern of epic poets that began in the *Iliad* with the "catalogue" of ships and commanders engaged in the Trojan War. Formidable as the many unknown names may seem, the student need not be disturbed because he recognizes so few. While more of them would have been familiar to Milton's contemporaries, even they would have been impressed with the "learning" lying behind this passage. Some of Milton's sources have been suggested by Grant McColley in "The Epic Catalogue of *Paradise Lost*," (*ELH*, IV (1937) 180-91) but apart from specific sources to which the blind poet must have referred his amanuensis, Milton here as elsewhere loved long passages of proper names, both for their sound and for their evocation of legend and lore.

For our purposes, it will be enough to stop over a very few of the fallen angels, either those of whom we have heard before or those we shall meet again. Notice the point Milton makes before he begins to recite the "catalogue." These names were not the names the angels had borne in Heaven. Those we shall never know,

> Though of their names in Heavenly records now
> Be no memorial, blotted out and razed
> By their rebellion from the Books of Life.
>
> (I. 361-63)

Nor had some of the former angels as yet taken on various names by which they were to be known among "the sons of Eve"—false gods, idols, worshiped by men in place of the true God.

About half-way through the catalogue, Milton introduces one false god of whom we have already heard in the *Nativity Ode*— Dagon, the "twice battered god of Palestine." In lines 457-466 Milton repeats the story that the "captive ark Maimed his brute image. . . . Where he fell flat, and shamed his worshipers." But the two most important characters in the catalogue are those to whom Milton gives the prominence of the first and last place, Moloch and Belial. We shall understand why they hold these places better after we see and hear them in the Council Scene in Book II.

> First Moloch, horrid king, besmeared with blood
> Of human sacrifice, and parents' tears.

Moloch was a primitive deity, worshiped by primitive peoples. His worship was accompanied by blood-sacrifice, particularly of children, whose cries were concealed by the roll of drums and the loud clash of timbrels. Essentially a simple deity, he was associated with violence, savagery, cruelty and noise. At the opposite extreme is the last fallen angel mentioned in the catalogue (ll. 490-505)

> Belial came last, than whom a spirit more lewd
> Fell not from Heaven, or more gross to love
> Vice for himself.

Moloch appeared early, Belial late in human history. Belial is a god of highly sophisticated men living in periods of decadence. He is not worshiped in a particular temple or at a smoky altar. When he is found at an altar, indeed, it is not in his own shape but "when the priest Turns atheist." His followers are in courts, in palaces, in luxurious cities—the Sodoms and Gomorrahs of any period of sophisticated degeneracy—degenerate and decadent men, often with unnatural vices. Moloch had a real history as a demon-god, since he had been worshiped by the Ammonites, and, under the name of Chemosh, by the Moabites. He was mentioned in the Old Testament (II Kings XXIII. 10) in connection with child-sacrifice. Belial, on the other hand, was never a real character but a personification. The word meaning "worthlesssess" was used in the Old Testament to imply evil, particularly lust. Before Milton made him a living character, he had occasionally appeared in medieval literature as a type of sensuality.

In the meantime we should add one other "speaking character" who will appear in the Council Scene, whom Milton did not mention in the catalogue since he had reason to introduce him in another way. Mammon is the leader of the band of "pioneers" who dug into the sulphuric earth for gold and other metals from which to build Pandemonium:

>   Mammon led them on:
> Mammon, the least erected Spirit that fell
> From Heaven, for even in Heaven his looks and thoughts
> Were always downward bent, admiring more
> The riches of Heaven's pavement—trodden gold—
> Than aught divine or holy else enjoyed

In vision beatific. By him first
Men also—and by his suggestion taught—
Ransacked the center, and with impious hands
Rifled the bowels of their mother Earth
For treasures better hid.

(I. 678-88)

Like Belial, Mammon was a personification rather than a legendary or historical devil. The word meant "wealth" in Syriac, and became familiar in the New Testament, particularly through Matthew's use of it (VI. 24): "Thou canst not serve both God and mammon." (Cf. Luke XVI. 9, 11, 13): Milton's Mammon is a thoroughgoing materialist. We shall come to know each of these fallen angels more intimately in the Council Scene, and hear of some of them again in connection with the battle in Heaven.

BOOK II

The Council Scene

In Book II we sit comfortably within the walls of Pandemonium, hardly conscious of the "darkness visible," the smoke and stench, the physical discomforts of the first Hell. While the great majority of the fallen angels remain within the "temple" of St. Peter's, a smaller group—though even they number one thousand—met in conference in the adjoining building to take part (like their ancestors in the *Iliad* or the *Aeneid*) in a council to determine plans of strategy. This, too, is a magnificent hall, accommodating "a thousand demigods on golden seats" with Satan as their center:

High on a throne of royal state, which far
Outshone the wealth of Ormus or of Ind,
Or where the gorgeous East with richest hand
Showers on her kings barbaric pearl and gold,
Satan exalted sat.

(II. 1-5)

As chairman, Satan opens the meeting. Notice that—as nearly always—he addresses his compatriots by their former titles, "Powers
and Dominions, Deities of Heaven." As commander-in-chief it is
essential for Satan to make his followers feel that, though they have
lost a battle, they have not lost the war. "I give not Heaven for
lost," he declares. We will return "to claim our just inheritance."
This council has been called for deliberation:

by what best way,
Whether of open war or covert guile,
We now debate. Who can advise may speak.

(II. 40-42)

We must read the Council Scene on various levels. The anti-
Catholic satire of the "secret conclave" of the College of Cardinals
in the Vatican, is not stressed, except in a few passing phrases.
There are reminiscences, as I have suggested, of council scenes in
classical epics. But one matter we must bear constantly in mind.
Milton had lived through a period of war and the inevitable after-
math of war and reconstruction. As a servant of the State, he had
been present at various councils and intimately familiar with others, both within and without the Houses of Parliament. The Council scene has a "political level" which can be paralleled again
and again in later periods, particularly in our own troubled century, in London, Paris, Rome, Washington, in Geneva or the
United Nations. From his first-hand knowledge, as well as his wide
reading, Milton knew that whenever a council was called to consider such emergencies as those faced by Satan and the fallen angels, certain positions or "platforms" would be expressed and up-
held by certain types of men. Expert rhetorician as he was, Milton

adapts the speech of each one to his own particular nature. Each speech is a masterpiece of the oratory in which Milton had had long training. It would not surprise me to discover that each of them (like the *Areopagitica*) was based upon a real model among classical orators or historians. The speakers rise in an order which is far from fortuitous, involved as it is in the psychology of each speaker.

As Moloch had been the first to appear in the procession of demons, so he is the first on his feet when Satan declares the meeting open. We have heard that he was a primitive deity, worshiped by primitive people with blood-sacrifice. Milton now introduces him as "the strongest and the fiercest Spirit That fought in Heaven, now fiercer by despair." Somewhat like Shakespeare's Hotspur, Moloch, "rather than be less Cared not to be at all." His rhetoric is entirely consistent with his character. He does not address the chair or his colleagues. He plunges abruptly into his speech and gives his position in the first six words, "My sentence is for open war." If there was a table before him in the council chamber, I am sure he pounded on it. For wiles and guile he has as little inclination as for parliamentary procedure or subtle flattering of his colleagues. Let us *do* something and *do it now*. To the Molochs of this world, the answer is a simple one: "Let's fight." Moloch sees no problem in getting back to heaven in order to fight again. The natural motion of angels, he reminds the Council, is *up* (lines 75-82). Only by force were they pushed down to Hell. (Moloch might have pointed out, as we learn later, that God was quite aware that even fallen angels retained their natural "proper motion," since He caused a roof to be placed over Hell, presumably to keep the angels down.) Getting back to Heaven, then, is no problem to simple-minded Moloch. Once there, they will fight. Either they will be victorious or the Torturer (notice that Moloch and the other fallen angels refuse to say "God" and use various circumlocutions to avoid the word) will destroy them, so that they will be "quite abolished, and expire"—a fate far preferable to Moloch to the forced inactivity and ignominy of remaining vanquished in Hell.

Moloch concludes as abruptly as he began: "Which if not victory is yet revenge."

Hardly is Moloch seated than Belial rises, though not in apparent haste. A greater contrast could not be imagined between two speakers. Moloch "ended frowning," again undoubtedly pounding that hypothetical table or striking his prize-fighter hands together. Belial is dignified, suave, "graceful and humane." "A fairer person lost not Heaven." As an orator he is superb, as a disputant so adept that he can confuse any antagonist by apparent logic that is really sophistry:

> his tongue
> Dropped manna and could make the worse appear
> The better reason, to perplex and dash
> Maturest counsels.
>
> (II. 112-115)

His speech is almost twice as long as Moloch's and a marvel of casuistry. He is as conscious of parliamentary procedure, of "audience psychology" and of oratorial art as Moloch was impervious to all three. Belial has a most important reason for rising just when he does. He gives the audience no opportunity to respond to Moloch's program of action and fighting. The last thing decadent Belials want is activity and hardship. As an orator should, he addresses his peers. To those who may share Moloch's desire for action and revenge, he is careful to say that he, too, desires vengeance, that he is "not behind in hate." He would be the first to move for war, were it not. . . . And then comes a series of, "buts"—questions, quibbles, logical hair-splittings by means of which Belial, the subtle disputant, confuses all the issues, and reduces to nonsense the whole platform proposed by simple Moloch. He makes the audience aware of the insuperable difficulties involved in a proposal of war. It would be no such simple process as Moloch implied for the fallen angels to get back to Heaven (129 ff.). Angelic sentries and scouts are everywhere on guard. And even could they force their way back, what then? Here Moloch enters into the kind of

philosophical and theological questions that would never occur to
a Moloch: the nature of deity (137-142) which

> would soon expel
> Her mischief, and purge off the baser fire.

What then? "Our final hope Is flat despair." The possibility of total annihilation was one thing to Moloch; it is quite another matter
to the highly intellectual Belial:

> Sad cure! for who would lose
> Though full of pain, this intellectual being,
> Those thoughts that wander through eternity,
> To perish rather, swallowed up and lost
> In the wide womb of uncreated Night,
> Devoid of sense and motion?
>
> (II. 146-151)

As Moloch reminds me of Hotspur, I wonder whether there are
overtones of Hamlet in Belial? Critics have suggested parallels between these lines and some of Claudio's in *Measure for Measure,*
but *Hamlet* was in Milton's conscious memory later in Belial's
speech, when in line 185 he paraphrased Shakespeare's "un-
houseled, disappointed, unanealed" with three other negatives,
"unrespited, unpitied, unreprieved." In lines 151-158 Belial returns again to the philosophical question of the nature of deity,
suggesting an argument of scholastic logic over which I will not
pause at present, since I shall discuss it in a more important context
in Adam's soliloquy in Book X. All this philosophy and theology
must have confused Moloch so much that, as Belial intended, he
would never have ventured a rebuttal. Is this really the worst fate
that could befall us? asks Belial (lines 163-186)? Here in this magnificent building, he implies, are we not physically far better off
than when we were struck by the thunder of Heaven, when we lay
chained on the burning lake? The tortures we have already experienced may prove as nothing in comparison with those with
which the Victor might "arm again His red right hand to plague
us." No, let us not talk of further war; for the present let us be glad

to remain where we are. (Belial is very comfortable in Pandemonium and physical comfort is the first desideratum of Belials.) His program is largely negative—what not to do, rather than what to do. In so far as he proposes a more positive one, it is curiously reminiscent of a phrase my generation remembers well from the First World War—"watchful waiting." (ll. 208-225) Let us wait and watch and see what happens, and in the meantime do nothing but enjoy ourselves as much as we can.

> Thus Belial, with words clothed in reason's garb,
> Counselled ignoble ease and peaceful sloth,
> Not peace.
>
> (II. 226-228)

Mammon rises next. Belial has prepared the way for him, for the Mammons and the Belials have much in common. The Mammons want war only for the material gain it may bring them, not for arduous labor and physical suffering. Indeed the Mammons have always proved most successful "draft dodgers," pleading their great value behind the scenes. Mammon does not want war, nor does he wish to return to Heaven for indefinite eons of "warbled hymns" and "forced hallalujahs." "How wearisome Eternity so spent." In this way, he is at one with Belial (lines 229-49). But he has a more specific plan to propose than had Belial. Instead of talking further about the possibility of storming Heaven, let us

> rather seek
> Our own good from ourselves, and from our own
> Live to ourselves though in this vast recess,
> Free, and to none accountable, preferring
> Hard liberty before the easy yoke
> Of servile pomp.
>
> (II. 252-57)

Expressed thus, Mammon's position momentarily sounds lofty, even noble in its contrast between the servility of Heaven and the "hard liberty" of Hell, particularly when he goes on to urge the fallen angels to work together in such a way that they will "thrive under evil and work ease out of pain Through labor and endurance." Almost he persuades us of his high-mindedness—almost, but not quite, when we come to the specific plan he proposes:

> This desert soil
> Wants not her hidden luster, gems and gold;
> Nor want we skill or art from whence to raise
> Magnificence, and what can Heaven show more?
>
> (II. 270-73)

To Moloch Heaven is only a *place*—a place with golden pavements, handsome buildings encrusted with more precious jewels than even those in Aaron's ephod. During the short time they have been in Hell, the "pioneers" under his direction have built Pandemonium, rivalling in magnificence any edifice in Heaven. Mammon's eyes seem to sparkle like those precious gems as he anticipates the building of another metropolis, far more splendid than the City of Heaven. It has not taken him long to estimate cannily the natural resources of the new world into which he has fallen.

Mammon's platform sounds even more reminiscent than Belial's to some of our modern ears. He says in effect: we have all the natural resources; let us seek our own good from ourselves. Was there not a period in fairly recent American history when some men urged a platform of "self-sufficiency?" "Free and to none accountable"—did we once hear about "no entangling alliances?"

> Nor want we art and skill from whence to raise
> Magnificence; and what can Heaven show more?

For "Heaven," read "Europe"; transfer the locale, and we may possibly have a platform once called "America first."

Milton has not told us of the audience-reaction to either Moloch or Belial. There is no question of the applause received by Mammon:

> He scarce had finished when such murmur filled
> The assembly, as when hollow rocks retain
> The sounds of blustering winds . . .

> such applause was heard
> As Mammon ended, and his sentence pleased . . .
>
> (II. 284-91)

Not only do most of the fallen angels dread another war, but, venal as they are and nationalists at heart, they have no less desire than Belial

> To found this nether empire which might rise
> By policy and long process of time
> In emulation opposite to Heaven.
>
> (II. 295-97)

Satan has undoubtedly been following all the speeches with the closest interest. The enthusiastic reception of Mammon's platform is momentarily disturbing, since Satan has a very different platform of his own which he intends shall be carried. Beelzebub, his spokesman, has been watching the meeting as carefully and knows that the time has come to divert the attention of the council from Mammon. Next to Satan in Heaven, Beelzebub is the vice-regent in Hell, a Prime Minister to the monarch, a statesman *par excellence,* in appearance, manner and oratory fully worthy his exalted position:

> with grave
> Aspect he rose, and in his rising seemed
> A pillar of state: deep on his front engraven
> Deliberation sat, and public care;
> And princely counsel in his face yet shone,
> Majestic through in ruin. Sage he stood,
> With Atlantean shoulders fit to bear
> The weight of mightiest monarchies; his look
> Drew audience and attention still as night
> Or summer's noontide air, while thus he spake.
>
> (II. 300-309)

Like Satan he addresses his colleagues by the titles they had borne in Heaven, then ironically warns them that, if they continue as they seem to be going, they will change those honored titles for "Princes of Hell." In the first part of his speech, he replies in effect to the three previous speakers: Moloch's simple, "I want war"; Belial's, "I want to stay here in peaceful sloth"; Mammon's, "I want to build a rival kingdom." All would prove equally unrealistic in the eyes of the King of Heaven (notice again the circumlocution). Clearly no one can win against omnipotence and any attempt on our part to rival His kingdom will meet with an "iron scepter" that has replaced the golden one with which he ruled over us in Heaven, "custody severe And stripes and arbitrary punishment." There is no weak spot in the armor of such a King. But in a very different way we may achieve the revenge we all desire. Beelzebub goes on to tell the fallen angels of something most of them did not know: in place of the third part of angels who fell, the heavenly Conqueror intends to create another world and a "new race called Man," to love Him, to serve Him, and in time to replace in Heaven the angels who rebelled. Far greater revenge than any so far proposed will be ours if we can find this new world, and either drive out the inhabitants as we were driven out, or, better still,

> Seduce them to our party, that their God
> May prove their Foe, and with repenting hand
> Abolish his own works. This would surpass
> Common revenge and interrupt His joy
> In our confusion, and our joy upraise
> In His disturbance: when his darling sons,
> Hurled headlong to partake with us, shall curse
> Their frail original, and faded bliss—
> Faded so soon.
>
> (II. 368-76)

Beelzebub's—actually Satan's—plan is eminently practicable and involves the only kind of revenge possible against an omnipotent deity who can never be defeated by physical strength—the seduction by force or guile of the new race God has created to serve and love Him and in time to replace the rebel angels.

> The bold design
> Pleased highly those infernal States, and joy

Sparkled in all their eyes; with full accord
They vote.

(II. 386-89)

Beelzebub has interrupted himself only momentarily. He rises again with the deliberate intention of building up in the imaginatons of his listeners the almost incredible difficulties that will be encountered by anyone—and this is a one-man mission—who undertakes to find the new world and the new race. All this, obviously, so that Satan's volunteering, which Beelzebub knows is coming, will seem as courageous and dramatic as it needs to be. Let us give the devil his due; the mission is really as perilous and hazardous as Beelzebub makes it seem. When we begin to follow Satan on his cosmic voyage, let us remember the passage in which Beelzebub for the first time suggests the new sense of vastness and space that was being felt in the seventeenth century:

> But, first, whom shall we send
> In search of this new world? whom shall we find
> Sufficient? who shall tempt with wandering feet
> The dark unbottomed infinite Abyss,
> And through the palpable obscure first find out
> His uncouth way, or spread his airy flight,
> Upborne with indefatigable wings
> Over the vast abrupt ere he arrive
> The happy isle? What strength, what art can then
> Suffice, or what evasion bear him safe
> Through the strict sentries and stations thick
> Of angels watching round? Here he had need
> All circumspection, and we now no less
> Choice in our suffrage—for on whom we send
> The weight of all, and our last hope, relies.

(II. 402-416)

The stage is set. The breathless audience, appalled at the dangers, "sat mute." Satan rises to the dramatic moment which he has so consciously prepared through Beelzebub. He too stresses the dangers and difficulties of the mission, beginning with a paraphrase